C000244949

# Alcohol Not Included

JASSY DAVIS
Illustrated by Bett Norris

# Alcohol Not Included

Alcohol-free
Cocktail Recipes for
the Mindful Drinker

HarperCollins*Publishers*

Dedicated to Francesca Burnett-Hall, whose experiments in dry drinking inspired me to get sober curious.

Thank you to Bett Norris for illustrating the recipes so beautifully, and to my editor Caitlin Doyle for kindly and patiently steering me through the process of writing this book. Thank you to Lucy Sykes-Thompson for her superb design, and to Helena Caldon, Rachel Malig, Abi Waters, Jacqui Caulton, Helen Rochester, Alan Cracknell, and Ben Murphy for helping to create our lovely book.

---

HarperCollins*Publishers*
1 London Bridge Street
London SE1 9GF
www.harpercollins.co.uk

HarperCollins*Publishers*
Macken House, 39/40 Mayor Street Upper
Dublin 1, D01 C9W8, Ireland

First published by HarperCollins*Publishers* in 2020

10 9 8 7 6 5 4 3 2


Written by Jassy Davis
Illustrated by Bett Norris
Designed by Lucy Sykes-Thompson

A catalogue record for this book is available from the British Library

ISBN 978-0-00-843422-9

Printed and bound by Oriental Press, Dubai

# Introduction

A lot of us are choosing our drinks from the alcohol-free section of the bar menu these days. Not necessarily because we're committed, year-round dry drinkers – although plenty of people are enjoying a teetotal lifestyle – but because we're sober curious. We want the exciting flavours, the elegance, and the glamour that modern cocktails deliver, just without the hangover.

Lucky for us, the world of soft drinks is changing. Boring lime sodas and old-fashioned Shirley Temples have been banished. In their place are a range of 'nolo' (no- and low-alcohol) drinks that take in a global pantry of ingredients and match them with contemporary cocktail techniques.

Inspired by this zero-proof revolution, the collection of non-alcoholic cocktails, long drinks, punches, and pitcher drinks in this book will help you craft your perfect spirit-free sipper – whether that's a stylish short served on the rocks or an indulgent dessert drink to round off a meal.

There's a shopping guide (see pages 11-13) that will help you get to grips with the amazing array of ingredients you can use to whip up a non-alcoholic cocktail, and a how-to section that takes you through the bar tools, kitchen equipment, and glassware you'll need to mix and serve a chic booze-free drink (see pages 7-10). If you really want to elevate your homemade cocktails, the Mocktail Cabinet (see pages 14-21) is stocked with base recipes for heritage soft drinks, including syrups, shrubs, cordials, and switchels, that'll help you level up your spirit-free cocktails and turn them into something special.

Whether it's one zero-proof drink or a whole lifestyle you're after, this book has got you covered. The sober end of the bar menu is finally fun, and these recipes will help you recreate that deliciously alcohol-free vibe at home.

# Bar Equipment & Stemware

## Building A Bar

Crafting mixed drinks doesn't take a lot of special equipment; you can shake drinks in a jam jar or simply stir them with ice cubes in a jug with a tablespoon. But there are a few tools that will make your life easier, and some that are just fun to have. This is a short guide to the bar tools, kitchen equipment, and glassware you might want to invest in to take your zero-proof cocktails to the next level.

### IN THE KITCHEN

To get started and prepare the ingredients for your drinks, you will need a few key pieces of equipment.

**Blender**
A solid, heavy-duty blender that can crush ice as well as blitz fruit into a pulp or whizz ice cream into a milkshake is always a good buy.

**Scales**
Digital scales are useful for weighing ingredients for making cordials, shrubs and syrups. If you have a very steady hand, you can put your glass or shaker on the scales and weigh out small quantities of ingredients directly into it to make individual cocktails.

**Measuring jug**
A measuring jug should ideally be heatproof, for when you need to steep hot teas and tisanes. It is also great for measuring liquids for large drinks for a crowd.

**Mini measuring glasses**
A shot glass marked with millilitres, fluid ounces, teaspoons and tablespoons is every drink-maker's friend. Perfect for measuring out ingredients for single-serve drinks.

**Heatproof fine-mesh sieve**
This is useful for straining fruit or vegetable pulp out of prepared drinks and mixers, like the Pear & Rosemary Shrub (see page 18).

**Muslin cloth**
Line sieves with muslin cloth to finely strain out fruit and vegetable pulp. This extra layer prevents even the tiniest bit of pulp getting through, which could make the end result cloudy.

## ON THE BAR

Ingredients at the ready, it's time to get mixing. These are the essential items you'll need to create that perfect blend.

**Mixing glass and bar spoon**

A heavy-based mixing glass, finely etched, looks handsome on a bar and is perfect for mixing drinks together over ice. Just half-fill with ice, add the ingredients, then use a long-stemmed bar spoon to turn the ice and liquids until everything is ice cold. Bar spoons typically have a 2.5–5ml (½–1 tsp) bowl (handy for measuring small ingredients) and a twisted stem that makes them easier to grip.

**Jigger**

A jigger is an hourglass-shaped measurer that has a measuring bowl on each end – the standard jigger (45ml/1½fl oz) and the pony (30ml/1fl oz). These are the basic measurements for all cocktail making. A jigger is not as precise as a mini measuring glass, but it is useful to have around.

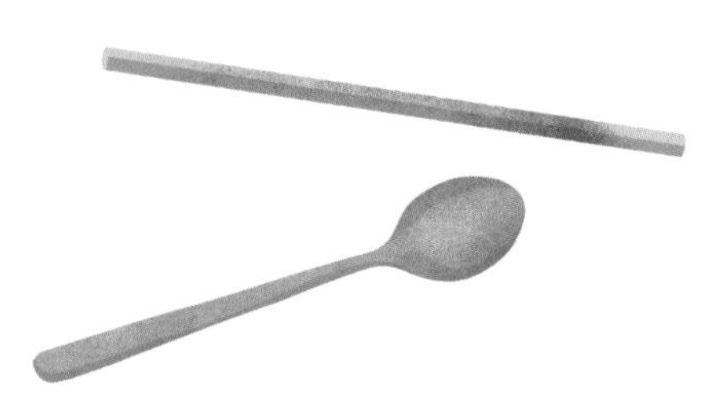

**Cocktail Shaker**

More glam than a repurposed jam jar, there are three basic types of cocktail shaker. The cobbler shaker is the three-part metal shaker you're probably most familiar with. It breaks down into a shaking tin, a fitted lid with a strainer built in, and a cap. It's the ideal choice for beginners who don't want to buy a separate strainer. The French shaker comes in two pieces and is shaped like the cobbler, but without the integral strainer. The Boston shaker is a two-piece shaker consisting of a large shaking tin (often metal) and a smaller shaking tin (often glass and called the pint glass). This shaker is a little trickier to use because you have to make sure you create a seal between the two tins before starting to shake, and it doesn't come with a strainer. The cobbler gets my vote for shaking drinks, unless you really want to add some flair to your cocktail making with a Boston shaker.

**Hawthorne strainer**

This strainer features a round disc with holes punched in it and spring running around one edge. They're designed to be a little smaller than most standard cocktail shakers and the spring will fit snugly inside your cocktail shaker's tin, providing stability when you tip the tin and pour the cocktail out. A hawthorne strainer is essential if you're using a Boston or French shaker. It will also come in useful if you're using a cobbler shaker to make cocktails with muddled fruit, as the integral strainer can get clogged with fruit pulp.

### Muddler

A muddler is a long-handled tool with a flat head that is used to crush soft fruits, extract essential oils from herbs and citrus peel and crack seeds and nuts. They're especially handy if you're making a lot of alcohol-free Mojitos. Muddlers are made from wood, metal, and plastic. Wooden muddlers are popular with bartenders because they're multipurpose, durable and look handsome, but they do stain easily. A metal or plastic muddler has the advantage of being easy to wash. Steel muddlers are all-rounders: great for crushing spices, extracting oils from herbs and citrus peels, and crushing fruit. If you mainly plan on bashing berries and citrus fruits for long drinks, then a plastic muddler is the one for you.

### Citrus juicer

A citrus juicer saves time and mess when you're squeezing lemons, limes and oranges.

## IN THE GLASS CABINET

After all that effort preparing your cocktail, serving it with a flourish is key. You want the right size and shape glass for your drinks for perfect presentation.

### Highball or Collins classes

These are the best glasses for long drinks, such as the Palomita (see page 27) and Lemon & Mint Fizz (see page 32). Highball glasses are tall and skinny, while Collins glasses are a little bit taller. The difference is minimal, so they can be used interchangeably. Look for glasses with a volume of around 35cl (350ml/ 12fl oz).

### Rocks glasses

These are lowball tumblers and they come in two basic sizes: single rock and double rock (also called the Old Fashioned glass). Single rock glasses are 25–30cl (250–300ml/ 8½–10fl oz) and they will comfortably fit a chunk of ice and your drink while still letting you slide in a bar spoon to give everything a spin. Double rock glasses are 30–35cl (300–350ml/ 10–12fl oz) and they make great midsize glasses for drinks, especially ones with crushed ice. They are my tumbler of choice for most of the short drinks served over ice in this book.

### Martini and coupe glasses

Classic V-shaped martini glasses are not currently fashionable, but they can be fun and must be due a comeback soon. Most zero-proof cocktails that are served 'up' (that is, not over ice) are poured into round-bowled coupe glasses. Whether you're buying a martini glass or a coupe, make sure they have a volume of 17cl (170ml/ 6fl oz) or up to 21cl (210ml/ 7fl oz) for larger drinks. The more generously sized martini glasses are also great for serving frozen Margaritas.

**Flutes and wine glasses**

You need flutes for elegantly sparkling drinks, like the Blackberry Royale (see page 143). These celebratory drinks wouldn't feel as special served in a wine glass. However, large wine glasses are useful for spritzes because, as you hold the glass by the stem, the drink doesn't get warmed up by your hand. This is especially important for ice-cold drinks like the Spritz Laguna (see page 62).

**Copa glasses**

An alternative to wine glasses for spritzes, copa glasses are bulbous, balloon-shaped glasses with a long stem that have been likened to fishbowls. Also called *copa de balon*, balloon glasses and gin goblets, copa glasses were invented in the Basque region of Northern Spain. The glass bowl is said to trap the drink's aromatics, so you can breathe them in and enjoy them more fully, as well as slowing down the rate at which ice melts – important for not diluting drinks, whether they contain alcohol or not. So always pack copas with ice when you're serving drinks like the Mountain Breeze (see page 86). The more ice in the glass, the slower your drink melts and the colder and more refreshing your drink will be.

**Margarita glasses**

A stemmed glass with a curved bowl, margarita glasses are a lot of fun but are optional – unless you are a die-hard, spirit-free margarita drinker. Margarita glasses tend to average out at 22cl (220ml/ 8fl oz), although you can get smaller margarita glasses that are comparable to a coupe as well as giant ones that are a bit like a stemmed bucket. You can use coupes and copas or wine and martini glasses for your margaritas if you don't want to invest in such a drink-specific glass straight away.

**Poco grande glasses**

Also called the Piña Colada glass, these large, curvy glasses with short stems are perfect for non-alcoholic Piña Coladas (of course), but also other frozen drinks and milkshakes. You can swap in a Collins or pilsner glass if you don't have any poco grandes in your glass cabinet.

**Pilsner glasses**

An elegantly fluted beer glass that typically holds 30–40cl (300–400ml/ 10–14fl oz), pilsners are great for non-alcoholic beer-based cocktails, like La Brava (see page 82), and also for big draughts of iced water or tea.

# Ingredients Shopping Guide

Most of the ingredients in this book are generally available in supermarkets, liquor stores, coffee supplies shops, delicatessens and – of course – online. But I find it helps to know what you're looking for in advance when you go shopping, so this is a guide to the drinks, pastes and flavour enhancers that I think are brilliant for making great alcohol-free mixed drinks.

**Aquafaba**
The viscous liquid found in cans of chickpeas. You can also make your own by cooking chickpeas, then draining them and keeping the cooking liquid. Aquafaba is starchy and can be whipped into a foam, which makes it a good substitute for egg whites in drinks (and meringues). Suggested as an egg substitute in Antheia's Cup (see page 31); G&Tea Sour (see page 39; Shake Shake Shake (see page 48); and Cold Brew Coffee Sour (see page 81).

**Barley tea**
A hot or cold infusion made from the roasted grains of barley. It has a nutty, toasted flavour, a little like digestive biscuits or graham crackers. Barley tea is particularly popular in Japan and Korea, and you can buy barley tea bags filled with ground, roasted barley for easy tea making. Turn to page 72 to read about some of the health benefits of drinking barley tea. Used in La Parisienne (page 72); and Blackberry Royale (page 143).

**Grenadine**
A tart syrup traditionally made from pomegranate juice and sugar with a dash of orange flower water. Modern grenadine syrups can be made from a mix of fruit juices, such as lemon, morello cherry and blackberry, as well as artificial flavourings to imitate pomegranate's tanginess. There are some great non-pomegranate grenadines on the market, but for a taste of the real thing look out for Jack Rudy Small Batch Grenadine or Liber & Co. Real Grenadine. Used in Kiss Me Quick (see page 93).

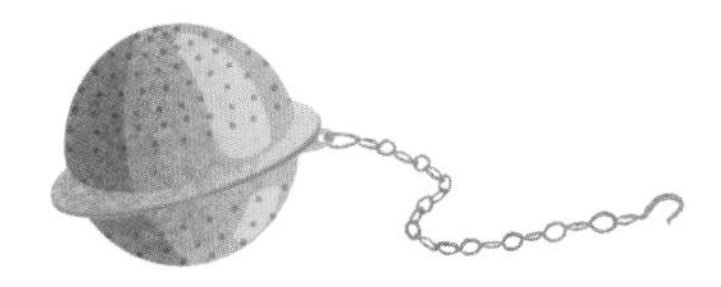

**Glycerine**
A clear, slightly viscous liquid that's used in baking to keep cakes moist or soften fondant icing – you'll find it in the baking section of your local store. In non-alcoholic cocktail-making glycerine adds texture. Alcoholic cocktails typically have a pleasantly soft mouthfeel, and that sense of the drink having body is often missing from non-alcoholic drinks. They're normally sharper, cleaner and thinner in texture. Adding glycerine thickens the drinks up a little, adding to their sippability. Throughout the book I have made glycerine optional – the drinks will be delicious with or without it. Experiment and see which way you prefer your spirit-free cocktails. Used in Antheia's Cup (see page 31); Kiss Me Quick (see page 93); Valentino's Kiss (see page 77); Buck's Twist (see page 106); Cold Brew Coffee Sour (see page 81); Up All Night (see page 85); Apple Mockatini (see page 117); Virgin Queen (see page 132); and Cat's Meow (see page 90).

**Jasmine tea**
A scented tea usually made with green tea leaves and jasmine flowers. The traditional process for scenting the tea has several stages: the tea leaves are picked, dried and then stored, ready for flavouring when the jasmine flowers blossom. The flowers are harvested during the hottest months of the year, at midday, to ensure they're in full bloom and heady with scent. The freshly picked jasmine flowers are mixed with the tea, which absorbs the flowers' perfume. This process can be repeated several times. However, modern methods of scenting the tea typically use jasmine flower oil or flavouring. Jasmine teas do go stale, so consume your tea within six months to a year of purchase. Used in G&Tea Sour (see page 39).

**Lapsang Souchong tea**
A black tea that originated in Fujian, China. The tea leaves are dried over pinewood fires to infuse them with the scent of the smoke. It's a very 'love it or hate it' tea and there is more information about it on page 89. Used in Peach & Basil Smash (see page 140); and Doctor's Orders (see page 89).

**Matcha tea**
Japanese green tea powder with a grassy, vegetal flavour. To read more about matcha's production and health benefits, turn to page 24. Used in Matcha Mojito (see page 24).

**Orange flower water**
Also called orange blossom water, it's a scented water made by steam-distilling orange blossoms. Most commonly used to flavour sweet treats like baklava, it has a strong floral flavour. A dash can beautifully perfume mixed drinks. Used in Lemon & Mint Fizz (see page 32); Shake Shake Shake (see page 48); Kiss Me Quick (see page 93); Buck's Twist (see page 106); and Midwinter Sparkler (see page 134).

**Pomegranate molasses**
A thick, sweet-and-sour syrup made by simmering fresh pomegranate juice until it's reduced and has an intense flavour. A key ingredient in Persian cookery, pomegranate molasses adds a citric bite to dishes and drinks that enhances the flavours. Used in Cold Brew Po-Groni (see page 54).

**Rose water**
An aromatic water made by either steeping rose petals in water or steam-distilling them, like orange blossom water. Rose water is often used in skincare, so make sure the rose water you buy is suitable for cooking. Also check the ingredients. Synthetic rose waters made with artificial flavours lack the luscious perfume of the real thing made with fresh rose petals. Use it sparingly to get the most out of its potent flavour. Used in Raspberry & Rose Refresher (see page 44); and Damask Fizz (see page 124).

**Tamarind paste**
A sour paste made from tamarind fruit. Tamarind is used to add bite and piquancy to dishes and drinks around the world, but especially in Mexico, India, China and the Caribbean. Tamarind fruit are quite fibrous, so they're often softened and pounded into a sticky paste before using, which makes a jar of ready-made tamarind paste a real time-saver. To read more about tamarind's health benefits, turn to page 52. Used in Frozen Strawberry & Tamarind Margarita (see page 52).

# The Mocktail Cabinet

When starting out as a dry drinks mixer, it can be helpful to have a store of interesting cordials, syrups, shrubs and switchels on hand. These alcohol-free concentrates are bursting with aromatics and they can act as a base note in your drinks, giving you a flavour foundation to build on. They're fairly easy to make and keep really well, so if you want to make them all and fill your fridge with spiced syrups and fruity cordials, you can. But if you're not sure which one you'll use the most, take a look at the relevant cocktails and start with the drinks that appeal the most.

## Simple Syrups

Simple syrups are made – very simply – from equal quantities of sugar and water boiled together until they form a light syrup. A basic simple syrup is made with white sugar and water. It's straightforwardly sugary and it's useful for sweetening a drink without obscuring the other flavours.

You can use different sugars to create syrups with more interesting flavour profiles. Demerara (Raw) Syrup will add a background note of toffee and caramel to your drink, while Honey Syrup is mellow with a delicate fragrance.

Infusing a basic white sugar simple syrup with aromatics – such as cardamom pods, lavender flowers or fresh herbs – is a great way of layering flavours in a drink. I've given several suggestions for spiced or flavoured syrups, all of which are used throughout this book. Once you get into the swing of making syrups, try your favourite spice or herb and see how that works in different zero-proof cocktails.

The final option is to make a simple syrup with a sugar alternative to create a sugar-free version. I've used Xylitol, which makes a subtly sweet syrup. You can use it in exactly the same way as a standard simple syrup and it's brilliant infused with aromatics, too.

## SIMPLE SYRUP

**Makes about 450ml (16fl oz)**
250g (8¾oz) granulated sugar
250ml (8½fl oz) water

Tip the sugar into a pan and pour in the water. Set the pan on a medium-high heat and bring to the boil, without stirring. Once the pan is boiling, set your timer for 2 minutes. After 2 minutes, take the pan off the heat and let the syrup cool. Transfer to a sterilized jar or tub, seal and store in the fridge for up to 1 month.

Used in Girl Next Door (page 36); and Winter Cup (see page 137).

## SUGAR-FREE SYRUP

Xylitol is a sugar alcohol that occurs naturally in plants. It has fewer calories than standard table sugar and it doesn't raise blood sugar levels, which can be a health benefit. It works well in syrups and is a good sweetener. However, it's worth noting that ingesting large quantities of Xylitol can cause an upset stomach, so be mindful about the number of sugar-free drinks you're having – don't overindulge. It can also be harmful for dogs, so no sharing drinks with your pooches, please.

**Makes about 450ml (16fl oz)**
250g (8¾oz) Xylitol
250ml (8½fl oz) water

Shake the Xylitol into a pan and pour in the water. Set the pan on a medium-high heat and bring to the boil, without stirring. Once the pan is boiling, set your timer for 2 minutes. After 2 minutes, take the pan off the heat and let the syrup cool. Transfer to a sterilized jar or tub, seal and store in the fridge for up to 1 month.

Used in Matcha Mojito (see page 24); Cold Brew Coffee Sour (see page 81); and Midwinter Sparkler Punch (see page 134).

**Note:** If you are planning to make several batches of a drink for a party using this Sugar-free Syrup, it might be best to use Simple Syrup in a 1:1 swap.

## FLAVOUR VARIATIONS

Infusing your Simple Syrup or Sugar-free Syrup with herbs, spices and citrus is an easy way to add flavour to your drinks. All the infusions work in the same way: simply add your chosen aromatics to the pan with the water and sugar, then heat and let the sugar dissolve to make a syrup. Boil for a few minutes, then cool and strain. Discard the aromatics and store the infused syrup in a sterilized jar or bottle in the fridge. They will all keep for up to 1 month.

## CARDAMOM

Add 50g (1¾oz) lightly crushed cardamom pods.

Used in Coffee & Cardamom Julep (page 70); and Frozen Mango & Lime Margarita (see page 98).

### SICHUAN PEPPER

Add 20g (¾oz) Sichuan peppercorns.
Used in Lime & Sichuan Gimlet (page 61).

### FIVE-SPICE

Add 15g (½oz) fennel seeds, 15g (½oz) Sichuan peppercorns, 6 star anise, 20 whole cloves and 1 cinnamon stick.
Used in Carrot Colada (see page 10); and Let It Rain (see page 47).

### GIN BOTANICALS

Add 20g (¾oz) juniper berries, 10g (⅓oz) coriander seeds, 30 whole cardamom pods, lightly crushed, 1 long strip of lemon peel, 1 long strip of orange peel, and 2 large fresh rosemary sprigs.
Used in Shake Shake Shake (see page 48); G&Tea Sour (see page 39); and La Parisienne (see page 74).

### LAVENDER

Add 10g (⅓oz) edible dried lavender flowers.
Used in Earl Grey Mockateani (see page 57); and Garden Spritz (see page 97).

### MINT

Add 20g (¾oz) fresh mint sprigs.
Used in Lemon & Mint Fizz (see page 32).

### BASIL

Add 20g (¾oz) fresh basil sprigs.
Used in Give A Fig (see page 101); and Watermelon, Basil & Lime Agua Fresca (see page 130).

### GINGER

Add 50g (1¾oz) sliced fresh root ginger.
Used in Hot Ginger Fizz, (see page 105); and Fire & Ice (see page 118).

### DEMERARA (RAW) SYRUP

Demerara or raw sugar is a minimally processed sugar made from sugarcane. It has an earthy molasses flavour that pairs especially well with coffee- or barley-based drinks.

**Makes about 450ml (16fl oz)**
250g (8¾oz) Demerara (raw) sugar
250ml (8½fl oz) water

Tip the sugar into a pan and pour in the water. Set the pan on a medium-high heat and bring to the boil, without stirring. Once the pan is boiling, set your timer for 2 minutes. After 2 minutes, take the pan off the heat and let the syrup cool. Transfer to a sterilized jar or tub, seal and store in the fridge for up to 1 month.
Used in Tried & Tested (see page 51); Cold Brew Coffee Sour (see page 81); and Apple Mockatini (see page 117).

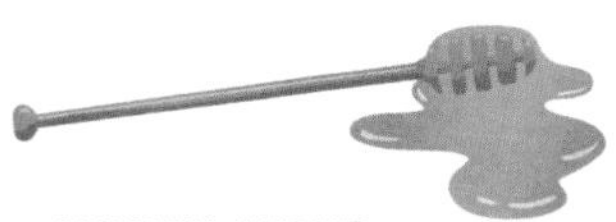

### HONEY SYRUP

The type of honey you use will affect the flavour of this syrup, so for an all-purpose syrup I like to use a blended table honey. This syrup is thinner than actual honey, so it's easier to mix into drinks, especially cold drinks shaken over ice.

**Makes about 450ml (16fl oz)**
250ml (8½fl oz) water
250g (8¾oz) honey

Pour the water and honey into a pan and set it on a medium-high heat. Bring to the boil, without stirring. Once the pan is boiling, set your timer for 2 minutes. After 2 minutes, take the pan off the heat and let the syrup cool in the pan. Transfer the syrup to a sterilized jar or tub, seal and store in the fridge for up to 1 month.

Used in Antheia's Cup (see page 31); Peach & Basil Smash (see page 140); Doctor's Orders (see page 89); and Cat's Meow (see page 90).

### CHOCOLATE SYRUP

This indulgent syrup is just as good drizzled over ice cream or pancakes as it is added to non-alcoholic drinks.

**Makes about 450ml (16fl oz)**
10g (⅓oz) cocoa powder
250g (8¾oz) granulated sugar
¼ tsp sea salt
250ml (8½fl oz) water
1 tsp vanilla extract or the seeds from ½ vanilla pod

Tip the cocoa powder, sugar, and salt into a pan and pour in the water. Set the pan on a medium-high heat and bring to the boil, stirring constantly. Keep your eye on the pan because it might try to over-boil – if it does, turn the heat down and keep stirring until it calms down. As soon as the pan is boiling, turn the heat down and simmer for 3–4 minutes. Take the pan off the heat and let the syrup cool. Stir the vanilla extract or vanilla seeds into the cooled syrup, then transfer to a sterilized jar or tub, seal and store in the fridge for up to 2 weeks.

Used in Mocha Mockatini (see page 114); and Earthquake (see page 69).

## Fruit Shrubs

Fruit shrubs are concentrated syrups made from fresh fruit, sugar and vinegar. They're also known as drinking vinegars and, while you can drink them straight up, shrubs are especially good turned into long drinks by mixing them with water (still or sparkling), tonic water or ginger beer. The two shrubs in this book both follow the standard 1:1:1 ratio of prepared fruit to vinegar and sugar, and I've used the hot method to make them. Shrubs can be cold extracted, with the fruit and vinegar mixed together and left for a week to infuse, then the mix strained and the liquid stirred with sugar to make a sweetened syrup. I like the hot method better just because it's faster (and I tend to forget things like bowls of fruit and sugar mellowing in a cupboard until it's too late and they've started to bloom) but if you have the time and the memory, give the cold method a go and see which you prefer.

### PEAR & ROSEMARY SHRUB

**Makes about 1 litre (1.7 pints)**

A squeeze of lemon juice
550g (19½oz) pears
350g (12oz) granulated sugar
350ml (12fl oz) cold water
1 heaped tbsp fresh rosemary leaves
350ml (12fl oz) white wine vinegar

Fill a bowl with water and add a good squeeze of lemon juice. Peel, core and chop the pears – you should have around 350g (12oz) chopped pears once you've finished. Pop them in the bowl of lemony water (this will help stop them going brown).

Tip the sugar into a pan and pour in the water. Set on a medium heat and gently heat until the sugar dissolves, stirring occasionally. Drain the pears, then add them to the pan with the rosemary leaves and bring to a gentle simmer. Pop on a lid and simmer for 6–8 minutes until the pears are soft. Pour in the vinegar and bring back to a simmer. Take the pan off the heat and let it cool for a few minutes, then strain the liquid through a sieve and into a jug. Press with a wooden spoon to squeeze out as much juice as possible. Discard the pears and rosemary. Pour the shrub into a sterilized bottle or jar, seal, let it cool, then store in the fridge. The shrub will keep for up to 2 months.

Used in Remember Me Always (see page 58); and Antheia's Cup (see page 31).

### RHUBARB SHRUB

**Makes about 1 litre (1.7 pints)**

400g (14oz) rhubarb
350g (12oz) granulated sugar
350ml (12fl oz) cold water
350ml (12fl oz) apple cider vinegar

Trim any dry ends off the rhubarb, then chop into small pieces – you should have around 350g (12oz) rhubarb once it has been trimmed and chopped. Set to one side. Tip the sugar into a pan and pour in the water. Set on a medium heat and gently heat until the sugar dissolves, stirring occasionally. Add the chopped rhubarb and bring to a gentle simmer. Pop on a lid and simmer for 8–10 minutes until the rhubarb is soft. Pour in the vinegar and bring back to a simmer. Take the pan off the heat and let it cool for a few minutes, then strain the liquid into a jug. Press the rhubarb pulp with a wooden spoon to possible. Discard the rhubarb. Pour the shrub into a sterilized bottle or jar, seal, let it cool, then store in the fridge. The shrub will keep for up to 2 months.

Used in Shanagarry Spritz (see page 40); and Damask Fizz (see page 124).

## Cordials

A cordial is made with a mixture of water, sugar, and fresh fruits or herbs. They're a traditional way of preserving fruits when there's a glut, such as soft berries in summer or citrus fruit in winter. They keep well in the fridge and are delicious just diluted with water, or used as an ingredient in a mixed drink.

### ELDERFLOWER CORDIAL

**Makes about 500ml (17fl oz)**
225g (8oz) fresh elderflower heads
225g (8oz) caster sugar
300ml (10fl oz) water

First, dunk your elderflowers in a big bowl of water and swirl them round to wash off any bugs. Drain the elderflowers and gently rinse again. Put the sugar and water in a large pan, then add the elderflowers. Cover with a lid and bring to the boil. Turn the heat down a little and simmer for 2 minutes, then take the pan off the heat. Leave to cool. Once the cordial in the pan is cold, strain it through a sieve into a jug. Pour into a sterilized bottle or jar. Store in the fridge for up to 2 months. To turn into a quick drink, pour 2 tablespoons cordial into a rocks glass over ice, add cold water and gently stir to mix.

Used in Shanagarry Spritz (see page 40); and Mountain Breeze (see page 86).

### RASPBERRY & THYME CORDIAL

**Makes about 250ml (8½fl oz)**
500g (17½oz) raspberries
2 tbsp fresh thyme leaves
120ml (4fl oz) cold water
100g (3½oz) caster sugar
1 tsp fresh lemon juice

Tip the raspberries and thyme leaves into a large pan. Add the water and place on a medium-high heat. Warm the raspberry mixture, stirring often, until it starts to bubble – be careful it doesn't boil over. Turn the heat down a little. Simmer for around 10 minutes, stirring occasionally, until the raspberries have collapsed and thickened a little. Set a heatproof, fine-mesh sieve over a heatproof jug. Pour the raspberry liquid through the sieve, then scrape and stir it with a wooden spoon until you have just the seeds and thyme leaves left in the sieve and a bright pink liquid in the jug. You should have around 200ml (7fl oz) raspberry liquid.

Pour the liquid into a clean pan and add the sugar. Put the pan on a low heat and gently warm, stirring, for 2–3 minutes until the sugar has dissolved (don't boil the liquid, keep the heat low). Stir in the lemon juice, then pour the cordial into a sterilized bottle or jar and seal. Store in the fridge for up to 4 weeks.

For a simple raspberry cordial, pour 1–2 tablespoons into a rocks glass full of ice and top up with chilled water.

Used in Raspberry & Rose Refresher (see page 44); and Raspberry & Thyme Cream Soda (see page 66).

### BLACKBERRY & BAY CORDIAL

**Makes about 200ml (7fl oz)**
500g (17½oz) blackberries
3 large fresh bay leaves
120ml (4fl oz) cold water
100g (3½oz) caster sugar
1 tsp fresh lemon juice

Tip the blackberries and bay leaves into a large pan. Add the water and place on a medium-high heat. Warm the blackberry mixture, stirring often, until it starts to bubble – be careful it doesn't boil over. Turn the heat down a little. Simmer for 10–12 minutes, stirring occasionally, until the blackberries have collapsed and the liquid has thickened a little. Set a heatproof, fine-mesh sieve over a heatproof jug. Pour the blackberry liquid through the sieve, then scrape and stir it with a wooden spoon until you have just the seeds and leaves left in the sieve and a rich purple liquid in the jug. You should have around 150ml (5¼fl oz) blackberry liquid.

Pour the liquid into a clean pan and add the sugar. Put the pan back on a low heat and gently warm, stirring, for 2–3 minutes until the sugar has dissolved (don't boil the liquid, keep the heat low). Stir in the lemon juice, then pour the cordial into a sterilized bottle or jar and seal. Store in the fridge for up to 4 weeks.

For a fast blackberry and bay drink, pour 1–2 tablespoons into a rocks glass full of ice and top up with chilled water.

Used in Blackberry & Ginger Cooler (see page 94); and Blackberry Royale (see page 143).

### BLUEBERRY & MINT CORDIAL

**Makes about 500ml (17fl oz)**
500g (17½oz) blueberries
20g (¾oz) fresh mint sprigs
120ml (4fl oz) cold water
100g (3½oz) caster sugar
2 tsp fresh lemon juice

Tip the blueberries and mint sprigs into a large pan. Add the water and place on a medium-high heat. Warm the blueberry mixture, stirring often, until it starts to bubble – be careful it doesn't boil over. Turn the heat down a little. Simmer for 8–10 minutes, stirring occasionally, until the blueberries have collapsed and the liquid has thickened a little. Set a heatproof, fine-mesh sieve over a heatproof jug. Pour the blueberry liquid through the sieve, then scrape and stir it with a wooden spoon until you have just the skins and mint sprigs left in the sieve and a rich purple liquid in the jug. You should have around 450ml (16fl oz) blueberry liquid.

Pour the liquid into a clean pan and add the sugar. Put the pan back on a low heat and gently warm, stirring, for 2–3 minutes until the sugar has dissolved (don't boil the liquid, keep the heat low). Stir in the lemon juice, then pour the cordial into a sterilized bottle or jar and seal. Store in the fridge for up to 4 weeks.

For a simple Blueberry & Mint Cordial, pour 1–2 tablespoons into a rocks glass full of ice and top up with chilled water.

Used in Blueberry & Mint Mojito (see page 102).

## Ginger Switchel

Switchel is a refreshing, non-alcoholic drink flavoured with ginger, sugar and vinegar. Its origins are unclear – possibly the Caribbean or China – but its heyday was the eighteenth and nineteenth centuries in the United States of America, when it was known as Haymaker's Punch because it was a popular thirst-quencher for farmhands. These days it tends to be made with maple syrup, as the liquid sugar blends easily in the drink and it adds the rich flavour of maple sap, along with raw apple cider vinegar for tang. It's delicious served over ice, either straight up or mixed with soda water, and it also works well in mixed drinks, where it adds some heat and flavour-enhancing tartness.

### GINGER SWITCHEL

**Makes about 1 litre (1.7 pints)**

50g (1¾oz) fresh ginger root
1 litre (1.7 pints) water
120ml (4fl oz) apple cider vinegar
150ml (5¼fl oz) maple syrup
1 tbsp fresh lemon juice

Scrub the ginger – you don't need to peel it – then slice it and tip it into a pan. Pour in the water, set the pan on a high heat and bring to the boil. When the water is boiling, take the pan off the heat and set aside to cool. When the ginger water has cooled, pour it into a sterilized jar. Add the vinegar, maple syrup, and lemon juice and stir to mix. Seal and leave to infuse in the fridge for at least 2 days and up to 5 days – the longer you leave it, the more fiery the ginger flavour will be. When it suits your taste, strain out the ginger, return the switchel to the jar or transfer to a sterilized bottle, seal and store in the fridge for up to 1 month.

### HOW TO STERILIZE JARS & BOTTLES

To sterilize glass jars and bottles, preheat your oven to 160°C/Fan 140°C/320°F/Gas Mark 3. Wash the jars and/or bottles in hot, soapy water (including the lids for the jars, if they have them), then rinse and place on a baking tray. Slide into the oven and heat for around 15 minutes. Take them out of the oven using oven gloves to protect your hands, add the syrup, shrub, cordial or switchel and seal. Remember the jars are hot, so let them cool before you transfer them to the fridge.

# Recipes

# Matcha Mojito

**SERVES 2**

1 tsp matcha powder
200ml (7fl oz) boiling water
2 lime wedges, plus extra to garnish
A handful of fresh mint leaves, plus sprigs to garnish
45ml (1½fl oz) Sugar-free Syrup (see page 15)
A dash of chilled soda water, to top up

**Matcha is good for you because...**

...it might help you focus. Matcha is a source of L-theanine, an amino acid that has been associated with improved cognition and attention, as well as feelings of calmness. So on stressed-out days a mid-morning matcha break could be just what you need to keep you on top form. Biscuits to go with the cuppa are optional.

**If a contemporary alcohol-free cocktail could ever be described as a modern classic, it's the Matcha Mojito. It combines the fresh flavours of everyone's favourite, cooling, Cuban, long drink with the Japanese green tea that has been all the rage for a few years now. Matcha means 'powdered tea' and it's made with green tea leaves that are covered up for three to four weeks before harvesting. This shade-growing technique forces the plant to produce more chlorophyll, making the leaves extra green, and it also preserves more of the amino acid L-theanine (more about that in the box). Matcha has a vegetal, spinach-like flavour, so a little goes a long way. If you're not sure just how grassy you like your mojitos, drop the matcha down to ½ teaspoon, then keep experimenting until you get the quantity right for you.**

Tip the matcha powder into a mug or heatproof jug and pour in the boiling water. Whisk to smoothly combine the tea, then set aside to cool. When you want to make the mojito, pop the lime wedges and mint leaves into a cocktail shaker and muddle or bruise them with a muddler or the end of a rolling pin. Add the Sugar-free Syrup and the matcha tea with a handful of ice cubes. Seal and shake well to chill. Add a handful of ice cubes to 2 Collins glasses, strain in the matcha mix through a hawthorne strainer or fine-mesh sieve. Top up with a dash of chilled soda water. Gently stir, garnish each glass with a wedge of lime and a mint sprig and serve with reusable straws.

# Palomita

**SERVES 1**

80ml (2¾fl oz) fresh ruby grapefruit juice
8ml (¼fl oz) unsweetened pickled gherkin brine, from the jar
15ml (½fl oz) fresh lime juice
8ml (¼fl oz) agave syrup
A dash of chilled soda water, to top up
Grapefruit wedge, to garnish

**This tall, tangy drink is based on the Paloma, Mexico's favourite cocktail. It's a citrus-heavy drink that, in its boozy form, features a kick of tequila. Finding a good, non-alcoholic swap for tequila required a little roundabout thinking. In the end I settled on a combination of agave syrup, for a hint of desert cactus sweetness, and the brine straight from a jar of pickled gherkins. Sounds weird, but it adds a tang that makes this drink deliciously refreshing. The brine's vinegary bite adds heat and also savouriness to the fruity mix of fresh grapefruit and lime juice. Unsurprisingly, this drink is brilliant paired with Mexican food. You can easily multiply the quantities and stir the drink over ice if you want to serve it to a crowd. If you do make a jug version, stir the grapefruit, lime, agave syrup and soda water together, then add half the brine, stir and taste. You may not need all the brine, or you may decide you want a splash more.**

Add a large handful of ice to a shaker and pour in the grapefruit juice, pickle brine, lime juice, and agave syrup. Seal and shake well to chill. Fill a tall Collins glass with ice cubes and strain in the Palomita mix. Add a dash of chilled soda water and gently stir together with a bar spoon until it's well mixed. Taste and add a little more soda if you think it needs it, then tuck in a wedge of grapefruit and serve straight away.

# Out of This World

**SERVES 1**

45ml (1½fl oz) pomegranate juice
45ml (1½fl oz) pineapple juice
45ml (1½fl oz) fresh orange juice
15ml (½fl oz) fresh lime juice
8ml (¼fl oz) orgeat syrup
Lime wedge and mint sprig, to garnish

The Mai Tai was invented in 1944 by Victor Jules Bergeron at his bar, Trader Vic's, in California. One night, friends from Tahiti came to visit Vic and he knocked them up a rum cocktail, mixing a fine 17-year-old rum with lime juice, curaçao, and creamy orgeat syrup. They took one sip and exclaimed: *Mai tai-roa aé!*, which is Tahitian for 'out of this world!' So naming this non-alcoholic version was nice and easy, although it meant that the drink had a lot to live up to. Luckily, it's delicious. A ruby-red long drink that's sticky with tropical fruit, sharpened by citrus, and with a smooth hint of almond thanks to the orgeat. It's a lot of fun and, while I've suggested a restrained lime wedge and mint sprig garnish, you could go all out with wedges of fresh pineapple, maraschino cherries, and – of course – a cocktail umbrella to honour the drink's tiki origins.

Add a large handful of ice to a shaker and pour in the pomegranate, pineapple, orange and lime juices, and orgeat syrup. Seal and shake well to chill. Fill a tall Collins glass with crushed ice then strain in the mocktail. Tuck in a lime wedge and a mint sprig to garnish.

# Antheia's Cup

**SERVES 2**

1 chamomile tea bag
150ml (5¼fl oz) boiling water
45ml (1½fl oz) Pear & Rosemary Shrub (see page 18)
15ml (½fl oz) Honey Syrup (see page 17)
30ml (1fl oz) egg white or aquafaba (the liquid from a tin of chickpeas)
1 tsp glycerine (optional)

**When I took my first sip of this sweet and refreshing drink, brimming with honeyed herbal flavours, I was reminded of the Greek island holidays I went on in my twenties, when I'd spend all day on the beach and then watch the sun set from a taverna terrace. The mix of chamomile tea with a pear shrub whisked me back to those white-walled courtyards with vine-covered arbours, pots of thyme and rosemary by the kitchen door, and the scent of mountain herbs in the air. I've named it after Antheia, the Greek goddess of flowers and blossom, whose symbol is honey and who was one of Aphrodite's servants. Antheia's blessing can help seal a marriage, so I've made sure this cocktail serves two.**

Pop the chamomile tea bag into a heatproof jug, pour over the boiling water and leave to steep for around 10 minutes, until the tea is nice and strong.

When you're ready to make the drink, fill 2 coupe or martini glasses with ice and set aside to chill for 5 minutes, or pop them in the freezer for 15–30 minutes.

Half-fill a shaker with ice and pour in the cooled chamomile tea, Pear & Rosemary Shrub, Honey Syrup, egg white or aquafaba, and glycerine if you're using it (glycerine adds texture to the drink, giving it body and a nice mouthfeel, but you don't have to use it). Seal and shake well for 30 seconds or so to chill. Strain into a clean glass or jug (not the coupe glasses), then pour the ice out of the shaker. Pour the mix back into the shaker, seal and dry shake for another 30 seconds to foam the egg white/aquafaba. Tip the ice out of the coupe glasses, then strain in the chamomile mixture and serve.

**Chamomile is good for you because...**

...it is believed to be a natural sleep aid. A 2005 experiment found that a chamomile extract helped sleep-disturbed rats doze off, while a 2016 study of new mothers showed that those who drank chamomile tea every day for two weeks slept better than the subjects who didn't. What works for rats and mums has got to work for the rest of us, right?

# Lemon & Mint Fizz

**SERVES 1**

35ml (1¼fl oz) Mint Syrup (see page 16)
22ml (¾fl oz) fresh lemon juice
½ tsp orange flower water
Chilled sparkling water, to top up
Mint sprigs, to garnish

Hottest day of the year? This is the drink to reach for. It was inspired by Limonana, a Middle Eastern mint lemonade that sprang into life as part of an advertising stunt in the 1990s. An Israeli advertising agency wanted to prove how effective its bus campaigns were, so they ran ads on the side of buses for 'limonana', a refreshing iced drink made from lemon (limon) and mint (nana). The ads created a huge buzz and, thrilled by the success of the campaign, the agency revealed it was all a hoax. There was no such drink. Except now, there was. So many people had gone into bars and cafés asking for a Limonana that people had begun creating their own. The drinks ranged from softly sparkling lemonades with a tingly hint of mint to bright green, brain-freezing slushies. This version is syrupy and heavy on the mint, which is perfect for when the sun is shining and the heat is rising.

Fill a Collins glass with ice cubes. Pour in the Mint Syrup, lemon juice, and orange flower water and gently stir to mix. Top up with chilled sparkling water, stir a couple of times, then tuck in a couple of mint sprigs to garnish. Serve with reusable straws, if liked.

# Caught in the Rain

**SERVES 2**

250ml (8½fl oz) coconut milk kefir
125ml (4fl oz) pineapple juice
150g (5oz) pineapple chunks, fresh or drained if from a can
15ml (½fl oz) fresh lime juice
Pineapple wedges, maraschino cherries, and cocktail umbrellas, to garnish

**Coconut milk kefir is good for you because...**

...it's a probiotic superhero. Kefir can contain up to 30 different strains of gut-healthy bacteria and yeasts. These 'friendly bacteria' can help ease digestion and improve symptoms like bloating. Each serving of kefir may contain millions of the little blighters, which is good news for overworked digestive systems everywhere.

**If you like drinking Piña Coladas, then you'll like getting Caught in the Rain. Sorry (not sorry), I can never resist an opportunity to quote 'The Piña Colada Song'. This virgin version of the beach-holiday classic is an indulgent treat. It's made with coconut milk kefir (more on that below), but you can swap in a standard dairy-based kefir or yogurt if you prefer, and crumble in a spoonful of coconut cream for that essential taste of paradise. It's a great cooler on hot days, and you can also turn the mix into ice lollies. Blend everything together, leaving out the crushed ice and swapping in 75ml (2½fl oz) Simple Syrup (see page 15), then pour into lolly moulds, insert sticks and freeze completely before enjoying.**

Pour the coconut milk kefir and pineapple juice into a blender. Add the pineapple chunks and the lime juice. Add a cup of crushed ice and blend together until smooth and creamy. Half-fill two poco grande or Collins glasses with crushed ice and pour in the pineapple and coconut mix. Garnish each glass with a wedge of fresh pineapple and a maraschino cherry speared on a cocktail pick and a cocktail umbrella.

# Girl Next Door

**SERVES 1**

**2 fresh passion fruits**
**75ml (2½fl oz) pineapple juice**
**15ml (½fl oz) fresh lime juice**
**15ml (½fl oz) Simple Syrup (see page 15)**
**½ tsp vanilla extract**
**Sparkling apple juice, to serve (optional)**

**A mixed drink with a heavy hint of the tropics about it, thanks to the heavenly combination of pineapple, passion fruit, and lime. One sip and you'll be whisked away somewhere warm, where the beaches have white sands and the skies are an endless blue. It's an excellent antidote drink to make in the depths of winter when the days are short, the nights long, and the weather bone-chillingly cold. It's cheering to drink something that tastes like a tropical island when you're missing the sun.**

Fill a large coupe glass with ice and set aside for 5 minutes to chill or pop it in the freezer for 15–30 minutes.

Halve the passion fruits, then scoop the flesh and seeds from three of the halves into a cocktail shaker (reserving the fourth half). Pour in the pineapple juice, lime juice and Simple Syrup. Add the vanilla extract and a handful of ice. Seal and shake well to chill. Tip the ice out of the coupe glass, then strain in the passion fruit mix through a hawthorne strainer (the integrated strainer in your shaker will get blocked by the passion fruit pulp, so use a hawthorne strainer or strain through a fine-mesh sieve). Float the remaining passion fruit half in the drink to serve. For the full effect, serve a shot glass of sparkling apple juice on the side, if you like.

**Passion fruit is good for you because...**

...it's rich in vitamin A. Each passion fruit contains around 8% of your daily recommended allowance of vitamin A. That might not seem like much, but passion fruit aren't very big, so they're packing quite a vitamin punch into a very small, easy-to-eat space. Vitamin A helps to keep your immune system fighting fit and your skin healthy.

# G&Tea Sour

**SERVES 1**

60ml (2fl oz) brewed jasmine green tea, cooled
30ml (1fl oz) fresh lemon juice
15ml (½fl oz) Gin Botanicals Syrup (see page 16)
1 tsp glycerine (optional)
15ml (½fl oz) egg white or aquafaba (the liquid from a tin of chickpeas)
A few drops of yuzu bitters, to serve (optional)

**Jasmine tea is good for you because...**

...it's high in antioxidants. Jasmine green tea contains antioxidants called catechins, which have been shown to reduce bacteria in the mouth, improving oral health and keeping bad breath at bay.

**I know I shouldn't play favourites, but this is the zero-proof cocktail I make the most. Light, floral and tangy, it tastes like a souped-up version of a lemon meringue pie. I've become so keen on it that when I make a jasmine tea in the morning, I pour out 60ml (2fl oz) and pop it in the fridge so I know I have it ready to shake up into a sour after work. When you're picking the tea for this sour, go for a good-quality green jasmine tea – it will make all the difference. There are two optional ingredients in the G&Tea Sour: glycerine and yuzu bitters. The glycerine gives the drink a thicker texture, replicating the viscous effect that alcohol has on cocktails. Without the glycerine, the G&Tea Sour is sharp, refreshing and easy to knock back. With the glycerine, it's a more elegant and sippable drink. The yuzu bitters (available from speciality liquor stores) add a finishing note of citrus, but they do contain alcohol. So if you're totally alcohol-free, leave them out.**

Fill a coupe glass or teacup with ice and set aside for 5 minutes to chill or pop it in the freezer for 15–30 minutes.

Half-fill a shaker with ice and pour in the cooled jasmine tea, lemon juice, Gin Botanicals Syrup, glycerine (if using) and egg white or aquafaba. Seal and shake well for 30 seconds or so to chill. Strain into a clean glass or jug (not the glass filled with ice), then pour the ice out of the shaker. Pour the mix back into the shaker, seal, and dry shake for another 30 seconds or so to foam the egg white/aquafaba. Tip the ice out of the glass or teacup and strain in the G&Tea Sour. If you're using the yuzu bitters, shake a couple of drops on top of the foam (a line of three drops looks pretty). Serve straight away.

# Shanagarry Spritz

**SERVES 1**

15ml (½fl oz) Elderflower Cordial (see page 19)
15ml (½fl oz) fresh lemon juice
45ml (1½fl oz) Rhubarb Shrub (see page 18)
A dash of soda water, to top up
Lemon slice, to garnish

A tall drink that tastes like spring and reminds me of the three months I spent at Ballymaloe Cookery School in 2010. Ballymaloe is located in the village of Shanagarry, on the south coast of Ireland. When I arrived the village was dotted with elderflower trees in blossom, while the school's kitchen garden had a rhubarb patch that was just starting to crop. On my first day in the kitchen I learned how to make poached rhubarb and fresh lemonade. Our teachers told us that if we wanted to make really delicious lemonade we should go and pick some elderflowers and use them to flavour the lemonade. After the lesson had finished, I sat in the canteen and gulped down glasses of ice-cold, floral-scented lemonade and ate a bowl of chilled rhubarb with whipped cream and shortbread. That magic combination of elderflower lemonade and delicately poached rhubarb stayed with me, and now, when I see the lacy sprays of elderflower appear in the trees and rhubarb begin to pile up on market stalls, I think of Shanagarry and Ballymaloe, and the amazing time I spent there.

Fill a Collins glass with ice cubes. Pour in the Elderflower Cordial, lemon juice and Rhubarb Shrub and gently stir to mix and chill. Top up with a dash or two of soda water, stir a couple of times, then drop in a lemon slice to garnish. Serve with reusable straws.

# Espresso & Tonic

**SERVES 1**

35ml (1¼fl oz) espresso, cooled
180ml (6fl oz) tonic water, chilled
Maraschino cherry, to serve

The first Kaffe&Tonic appeared on the menu of Koppi, a coffee roasters and café in Helsingborg, Sweden, in 2017. Espresso & Tonic quickly became their best-selling iced coffee and versions of the drink began popping up in cafés and bars around the country. Coffee is a big deal in Sweden – they consume over 8kg (18lbs) coffee per person every year – so a new way to get a caffeine fix was guaranteed to cause a stir. Eventually, the Kaffe & Tonic made its way around the world, helped by Instagram. The dark layer of espresso floating on top of a clear bubbly pool of tonic looks too good not to share. When you're making an Espresso & Tonic at home, use Fever-Tree Mediterranean Tonic Water if you can. It has less quinine in it and was developed to have a more fragrant herbal flavour than standard tonic water, making it light and bright and a good match for a slightly sour shot of espresso. To create the pretty two-tone effect, pour the espresso carefully into the tonic water. It should slowly drift down through the tonic water, giving you time to snap your Insta-friendly shot before sipping.

Make your espresso (or run to the coffee shop and get them to make one for you) and let it cool. Fill a Collins glass with ice cubes and pour in the tonic water. Gently and slowly pour the espresso into the glass over the back of a bar spoon, then drop in a maraschino cherry to serve.

# Raspberry & Rose Refresher

**SERVES 1**

45ml (1½fl oz) Raspberry & Thyme Cordial (see page 19)
1 tsp rose water
2 tsp orgeat syrup
150ml (5¼fl oz) sparkling water, chilled
Thyme sprigs, to garnish

**When I was little, my dad would take my sisters and me to the local sweet shop every Saturday night. We were allowed to buy a quarter pound of our favourite sweets. The shop shelves were lined with jars – cherry lips, fruit gums, toffee bon-bons, gobstoppers, strawberry laces and more. What has that got to do with this perfectly pink summer drink? Everything – the Refresher is like imbibing that sweet shop in a glass. Even better, it tastes like boiled sweets mixed with Turkish delight (my favourite). It's a joyous drink, bursting with fragrant raspberries and perfumed roses. The sparkling water gives it a sherbet fizz, adding to the nostalgic sweet-shop vibe.**

Fill a highball glass with ice cubes. Pour in the Raspberry & Thyme Cordial, rose water and orgeat and gently stir to mix. Top up with the sparkling water, stir a couple of times, then tuck in a couple of thyme sprigs to garnish. Serve with reusable straws, if liked.

# Let It Rain

**SERVES 1**

22ml (¾fl oz) fresh lime juice
15ml (½fl oz) Five-spice Syrup (see page 16)
150ml (5¼fl oz) ginger kombucha, chilled
Lime wedge, to garnish

This long drink is pure fun. A perfect Friday night drink, when you want to kick back, relax and abandon all the serious, grown-up things that make the working week so long. The Five-spice Syrup (see page 16) has an aniseed sweetness that reminds me of liquorice. Teaming it with a splash of lime juice and a good slug of ever-so-slightly sour ginger kombucha creates a mocktail that tastes a lot like sour jelly sweets – the mouth-puckering ones that are an addictive mix of sweet and sour. It's a tart, fizzy and playful drink. You can enjoy it by itself – or it's a great accompaniment to a juicy burger. The savouriness of the beef would pair nicely with the drink's syrupy side, while the kombucha's astringency would work well with any sweet-and-sharp pickles or rich cheese slices you pile into the burger bun. Remember that kombucha does usually contain a very small amount of alcohol due to the fermentation process, so for a totally zero-proof cocktail swap it for non-alcoholic ginger beer.

Fill a Collins glass with ice cubes. Pour in the lime juice and Five-spice Syrup and gently stir to mix, then top up with the chilled ginger kombucha. Stir a few more times to just mix it all together. Drop in a lime wedge to garnish. Serve with reusable straws, if liked.

# Shake Shake Shake

**SERVES 1**

22ml (¾fl oz) fresh lime juice
22ml (¾fl oz) fresh lemon juice
22ml (¾fl oz) Gin Botanicals Syrup (see page 16)
22ml (¾fl oz) single cream
½ tsp orange flower water
15ml (½fl oz) egg white or aquafaba (the liquid from a tin of chickpeas)
Chilled soda water, to top up
Orange wheel, to garnish

This drink was originally inspired by the Ramos Gin Fizz. A mix of sweet and sour with a fluffy texture, the Ramos Gin Fizz is one of the great cocktails to come out of New Orleans. Invented by Henry Charles Ramos in 1888, it was an immediate success. In fact, it was so popular that Ramos had up to 20 'shaker boys' working in his bar every night and the only drink they made was the Ramos Gin Fizz. Partly this was down to the drink's popularity, and partly because Ramos' method involved shaking the ingredients together for 12 minutes. You don't have to shake this zero-proof version for quite so long, although if you've ever really wanted to go wild with your cocktail shaking, this is the drink. When you pour the drink, make sure you keep it slow and steady – the fizz comes from pouring the gin-scented (but gin-free) mix into the glass at the same time as the soda water. Pour too quickly and it will foam up and spill. So be gentle and patient. The result is a creamy drink with an orange heart and dry finish. It's incredibly refreshing – ideal for hot nights and heatwaves.

Half-fill a shaker with ice, then pour in the lime and lemon juices, syrup, cream, orange flower water, and egg white or aquafaba. Seal and shake well for at least 30 seconds to chill. Strain into a clean glass or jug, then discard the ice in the shaker. Pour the mix back into the shaker, seal and dry shake for another 30-60 seconds to foam the egg white/aquafaba. Fill a Collins glass with ice cubes and get ready to juggle (figuratively speaking). Hold the shaker in one hand and a bottle of chilled soda water in the other. Slowly strain the gin fizz mix into the glass while simultaneously pouring in the soda water at the same pace. The drink will foam up, so keep pouring until the glass is two-thirds full. Let the drink settle and the fizz calm, then strain in the rest of the gin fizz mix. Tuck in an orange wheel and serve.

# Tried & Tested

**SERVES 1**

1 barley tea bag
1 tbsp shredless orange marmalade
150ml (5¼fl oz) boiling water
1 tsp Demerara (Raw) Syrup (see page 17), plus extra to serve (optional)
3–4 dashes of Angostura bitters (optional)

**A mocktail for fans of the Old Fashioned, this zero-proof short drink uses barley tea as a stand-in for whisky. Barley tea is made from roasted barley grains (either whole or ground) and it has a nutty, biscuity flavour with just a hint of bitterness. I use Japanese barley tea bags when I'm making mocktails, and steeping a tea bag in a small amount of hot water for at least 20 minutes really concentrates the flavour. It does also concentrate the bitterness, so adding a sweetener is key. Demerara (Raw) Syrup swirls in some toffee sweetness, while marmalade – made with bitter oranges – adds a little citrus bite. The result is complex and aromatic. I've included Angostura bitters as an optional extra, but they do contain alcohol, so for a truly zero-proof cocktail, leave them out.**

Pop the barley tea bag and the marmalade into a heatproof jug and pour in the boiling water. Stir a few times to dissolve the marmalade, then let the tea steep for 20 minutes so it is really strongly flavoured. Let it cool.

When you're ready to make the drink, add a handful of ice cubes to an Old Fashioned glass. Pour in the marmalade-laced barley tea and add the Demerara (Raw) Syrup. If you're using Angostura bitters, add those too. Stir well for around 1 minute to chill. Taste, add a little more Demerara (Raw) Syrup if you think it needs it, and serve straight away.

# Frozen Strawberry & Tamarind Margarita

**SERVES 2**

150g (5oz) strawberries
75g (2½oz) tamarind paste
30ml (1fl oz) fresh lime juice
15ml (½fl oz) agave syrup
75ml (2½fl oz) cold water
2 lime wheels, to garnish

**Frozen margaritas have been on drinks' menus since the 1950s, when the brain-freezing beauty of blending tequila, triple sec and lime juice with crushed ice was first discovered. It's a great summer holiday drink and a poolside favourite, and this frozen delight shares that accolade. It blends juicy strawberries with tangy tamarind to create a sweet-and-sour slushy that's perfect for sipping on sunny days. And because it's booze-free, you'll have no trouble saying 'a sweet-and-sour slushy for sipping on summer days' five times in a row, no matter how many margaritas you drink (please consume alcohol-free margaritas responsibly).**

Put two margarita or wine glasses into the freezer for 15–30 minutes to chill. Hull the strawberries and pop them in a blender. Add the tamarind paste, lime juice, agave syrup, cold water, and a cup of crushed ice. Blitz until smooth. Taste and add a little more tamarind paste, lime juice, or agave syrup if you think it needs it – it should be sweet, sour, and tangy. Pour into the chilled glasses and garnish each with a lime wheel.

**Tamarind is good for you because...**

...it contains polyphenols, which are compounds found in plants that can have health benefits. Tamarind paste is made from the pulp of the fruit that grows in pods on tamarind trees. The polyphenols in tamarind – flavonoids – have been found to help lower LDL cholesterol, which is the kind that contributes to fatty build ups in arteries and which may increase the risk of heart attacks. In a 2013 experiment, tamarind extract helped lower LDL cholesterol in hamsters and put them back on the path to perfect health. How the hamsters came to have such high cholesterol in the first place, we can only guess.

# Cold Brew Po-groni

**SERVES 1**

45ml (1½fl oz) cold brew coffee
45ml (1½fl oz) Seedlip Grove 42 or similar non-alcoholic distilled spirit
8ml (¼fl oz) fresh lime juice
15ml (½fl oz) Bitter Apéritif syrup
8ml (¼fl oz) pomegranate molasses
1 tsp glycerine (optional)
Orange slice, to garnish

In April 2020 Hollywood legend and mixologist dreamboat Stanley Tucci brightened the internet by sharing a video of himself demonstrating how to make a Negroni. Rather than stir it together on the rocks, Tucci shook his Negroni and served it up in a coupe glass because he thinks they're nice served that way. Who am I to argue with Stanley Tucci? Consequently, this zero-proof version is shaken, not stirred, and it's served in a well-chilled coupe. It's fruitier than its boozy counterpart, with a dry finish and a hint of chocolate from the cold brew coffee. The pomegranate molasses adds tang while the glycerine gives it a soft texture (you can leave the glycerine out if you prefer). One key ingredient is Bitter Apéritif syrup. Both Monin and Giffard sell bitter syrups that have all the flavour of Campari with none of the booze. You'll find them in speciality coffee and liquor stores, and online. Once you've assembled all your ingredients, there's only one thing left to do: shake it like Stanley Tucci.

Fill a coupe glass with ice and set aside for 5 minutes to chill or pop it in the freezer for 15–30 minutes. Half-fill a shaker with ice and pour in the cold brew coffee, Seedlip Grove 42 or other non-alcoholic distilled spirit, lime juice, Bitter Apéritif syrup, pomegranate molasses, and glycerine, if using. Seal and shake well. Tip the ice out of the coupe glass, then strain in the Po-groni. Garnish with an orange slice and serve.

**How to cold brew your coffee**

Cold brewing coffee is exactly what it sounds like: slowly steeping coffee grounds in cold water to extract their flavour. Fans of cold brew claim it's smoother than a regular filter or espresso and that you get more of the coffee bean's natural flavour. Like all things coffee, there's a lot of debate as to how to make the perfect cold brew. The ideal ratio of coffee to water ranges from 1:8 to a caffeine crazy 1:2, while steeping time is anything from 8 to 48 hours. I like to keep things simple, so I use 1 tablespoon of filter coffee grounds steeped in 300ml (10fl oz) cold water for 12 hours. Start with that and then experiment until you find the ratios and steeping time that works for you. Cold brew coffee will keep in a sealed jar or bottle in the fridge for up to two weeks, so if you're using it as an ingredient for mocktails, you can make a big batch and work your way through it.

# Earl Grey Mockateani

**SERVES 1**

1 Earl Grey tea bag or 2 tsp Earl Grey tea leaves
Boiling water, for brewing
45ml (1½fl oz) Seedlip Grove 42 or similar non-alcoholic distilled spirit
15ml (½fl oz) fresh lemon juice
22ml (¾fl oz) Lavender Syrup (see page 16)
1 tsp glycerine (optional)
Lemon twist, to garnish

**I've put the emphasis on the tea in this zero-proof martini by making Earl Grey the hero at the heart of this elegant little drink. Earl Grey tea is a blend of black tea that's infused with bergamot oil, which gives it a zesty fragrance. It's a good flavour mate with Seedlip Grove 42, a citrus-forward, distilled, non-alcoholic spirit that's part of a range of non-alcoholic gin alternatives. Grove 42 features blood orange, mandarin, lemon and ginger among its botanicals, giving it a juicy hint of orange and an uplifting kick of spice. The Seedlip range of booze-free spirits is becoming easier to find in supermarkets, grocery and liquor stores around the world, but if you can't find these, take a look at the non-alcoholic 'alts' available in your area. Companies like Ritual in America, Lyres in Australia, and Abstinence in South Africa all offer non-alcoholic distilled spirits that make a good alternative to gin.**

Make the tea by pouring boiling water over the tea bag or tea leaves in a mug and steeping for 4–5 minutes, then strain out the tea bag or leaves and leave to cool a little. When you're ready to make the mocktail, fill a coupe glass with ice and set aside for 5 minutes to chill or pop it in the freezer for 15–30 minutes.

Half-fill a shaker with ice cubes. Measure out 45ml (1½fl oz) of the cooled tea and pour it into the shaker. Add the Seedlip Grove 42 or other non-alcoholic distilled spirit, lemon juice, Lavender Syrup, and glycerine, if you're using it. Seal and shake well for 30 seconds or so to chill. Tip the ice out of the coupe glass, then strain in the mocktail, drop in a lemon twist and serve.

# Remember Me Always

**SERVES 1**

50ml (1¾fl oz) Pear & Rosemary Shrub (see page 18)
15ml (½fl oz) orgeat syrup
150ml (5¼fl oz) soda water, chilled
Rosemary sprig, to garnish

Rosemary has symbolized remembrance for thousands of years. Both poetically, in the form of the boughs of rosemary strewn across tombs to honour the memory of the dead – a custom that began in Ancient Egypt; to the more practical wreaths of rosemary that students wore in Ancient Greece in the belief that the herb's scent would help improve their recall during exams. Those old-world scholars may have been onto something, as more recent studies have suggested that inhaling the scent of rosemary can help boost memory. So, if you have an exam coming up or a work project that needs a little extra brainpower, mixing up this soothing long drink could give you the lift you need. And even if it doesn't, it's a deliciously delicate drink that mixes the floral flavour of a pear and rosemary shrub with a creamy dash of orgeat syrup.

Fill a tall Collins glass with ice cubes. Pour in the Pear & Rosemary Shrub and orgeat syrup and gently stir to mix and chill. Top up with the chilled soda water, stir a couple of times, then tuck a rosemary sprig into the glass to garnish, and serve.

# Lime & Sichuan Gimlet

**SERVES 1**

45ml (1½fl oz) Seedlip Spice 94 or similar non-alcoholic distilled spirit
22ml (¾fl oz) fresh lime juice
15ml (½fl oz) Sichuan Pepper Syrup (see page 16)
1 tsp glycerine (optional)

**The Gimlet is one of the original cocktails, invented in the seventeenth century as a way to get vitamin C into English sailors and save them from scurvy. In the twenty-first century scurvy is not so much of a worry, but we still appreciate a super-zingy, lime-forward cocktail. This zero-proof version is made with a gin alt, Seedlip Spice 94. It's a non-alcoholic distilled spirit flavoured with allspice, cardamom, lemon, grapefruit, oak, and cascarilla bark. This warmly spiced gin alternative pairs brilliantlywith lime juice. Add a peppery hit of heat from a Sichuan peppercorn-spiced syrup and you get a bright and zesty mocktail that'll really perk up your taste buds. A perfect pre-dinner treat. If you can't find Seedlip in your local store, look out for other distilled alcohol-free spirits that would make a good swap for gin in this recipe.**

Fill a small coupe glass with ice and set aside for 5 minutes to chill or pop it in the freezer for 15–30 minutes.

Half-fill a shaker with ice and pour in the Seedlip Spice 94 or other non-alcoholic distilled spirit, lime juice, Sichuan Pepper Syrup, and glycerine, if you're using it. Seal and shake well for 30 seconds or so to chill the mocktail. Tip the ice out of the glass, then strain in the Lime & Sichuan Gimlet and serve.

# Spritz Laguna

**SERVES 1**

75ml (2½fl oz) Sanbittèr Rosso, chilled
50ml (1¾fl oz) fresh grapefruit juice
75ml (2½fl oz) soda water, chilled
A scoop of lemon sorbet

A few years ago, on holiday in Florence, I came back to my apartment after a long day touring churches and galleries feeling hot and sticky. I crumpled onto a chair on the tiny balcony, fanned myself with museum leaflets, and complained about how impossible it was to cool down in the city heat. Amazingly, my holiday companion, Nicola, didn't smack me over the head for being an ungrateful Moaning Myrtle. Instead, she fixed us both Aperol Spritzes, but instead of ice she spooned in some lemon sorbet. It was a revelation. The bitter liquor and the sweet sorbet fizzed together to make the liquid equivalent of air conditioning. This is my zero-proof version of that magic drink, made with Sanbittèr Rosso and with a scoop of sorbet dunked in it, like a swimmer cooling down in an Italian lake. Sanbittèr is an alcohol-free Italian aperitivo with a strong herbal flavour upfront and a touch of syrup to finish. You can find it in supermarkets and delis. It's wonderful served with soda over ice, if you run out of sorbet.

Pour the chilled Sanbittèr Rosso into a gin copa or wine glass, then add the grapefruit juice and soda water and stir to mix. Drop in a scoop of lemon sorbet and serve.

# Metropolitan Elite

**SERVES 1**

45ml (1½fl oz) fresh orange juice
45ml (1½fl oz) cranberry juice drink
15ml (½fl oz) fresh lime juice
15ml (½fl oz) fresh lemon juice
15ml (½fl oz) grenadine syrup
1 tsp glycerine (optional)
Orange twist, to serve

Inspired by the 1990s favourite cocktail, the Cosmopolitan, this fresh and fruity drink is a balanced mix of sweet, crisp and dry. It features a trio of citrus juices – orange, lemon and lime – shaken with tart cranberry juice to create the Cosmo's mouthwatering flavour. To keep the sharpness at bay – and to bump up the pinkness – I've also added a spoonful of grenadine syrup. Grenadine is made from pomegranate juice. It's boiled down until it forms a thick syrup that's sweet, but still has a little bite. For a single serving, I think this drink is best shaken over ice with a touch of glycerine to thicken it up. It would, however, make a good brunch drink, but shaking individual cocktails can be tiring when you're trying to serve a crowd. So, if you like, you can make a jug instead – multiply the quantities but leave the glycerine out, stir over ice and serve in Old Fashioned glasses on the rocks with lime wedges to garnish.

Fill a coupe glass with ice and set aside for 5 minutes to chill or pop it in the freezer for 15–30 minutes.

Half-fill a shaker with ice and pour in all the fruit juices, the grenadine syrup and the glycerine, if you're using it. Seal and shake well for 30 seconds or so to chill. Tip the ice out of the glass, then strain in the mocktail. Garnish with an orange twist to serve.

# Raspberry & Thyme Cream Soda

**SERVES 1**

45ml (1½fl oz) Raspberry & Thyme Cordial (see page 19)
125ml (4fl oz) soda water, chilled
22ml (¾fl oz) single cream
Raspberries and thyme sprigs, to garnish

**Cream sodas are something I have a nostalgic fondness for, even though I don't think they were ever really part of my childhood. I think my parents may have drunk them when they were kids, sold in glass bottles by the Pop Man, who delivered fizzy drinks door-to-door like a sugar-crazed milkman. Cream sodas were first created in America in the mid-1800s, although their popularity really exploded in the 1930s when the invention of synthetic vanilla extract made it easy to create a fizzy drink that tasted like melted ice cream. This fresh version ditches the vanilla flavouring in favour of actual cream stirred with soda water and floated on top of a luscious layer of homemade Raspberry & Thyme Cordial (see page 19). It tastes likes raspberries and cream, eaten on a warm afternoon in a summer that promises to go on forever.**

Fill a highball glass with ice, then pour in the Raspberry & Thyme Cordial. Pour in the chilled soda water. Pour the cream over the back of a bar spoon into the glass, then gently stir the soda water and cream together, leaving the syrup undisturbed. You should get a white layer floating on top of a deep pink layer of raspberry cordial. Drop in a couple of raspberries and tuck in a small thyme sprig to garnish.

# Earthquake

**SERVES 2**

35ml (1¼fl oz) espresso, cooled
22ml (¾fl oz) Chocolate Syrup (see page 17)
250ml (8½fl oz) full-cream milk
100g (3½oz) vanilla ice cream
Dark chocolate, for grating

**This milkshake for grown-ups was inspired by the Mudslide, an indulgent pudding cocktail invented in the Cayman Islands by a bartender at the Wreck Bar & Grill. That cocktail mixes coffee, vanilla and chocolate together to make a decadent drink that is easy to replicate without the booze because, well, you don't need alcohol to make coffee, chocolate and vanilla taste delicious. The double shot of espresso adds a touch of sophisticated bitterness to the sticky mix of ice cream and chocolate syrup and keeps it from being too sweet. If you want to recreate an American diner vibe at home and need a drink you can dunk your fries in (trust me, it's delicious), then this is the milkshake for you.**

Pour the espresso, Chocolate Syrup and milk into a blender. Add the vanilla ice cream and a cup of crushed ice. Blend together until smooth and creamy. Pour the Earthquake mix into two poco grande or Collins glasses and grate over a little dark chocolate to garnish. Serve straight away with reusable straws.

# Coffee & Cardamom Julep

**SERVES 1**

90ml (3fl oz) cold brew coffee
22ml (¾flfl oz) Cardamom Syrup (see page 16)
1 tsp rose water

**If you track the history of the word 'julep' back far enough you end up at 'gulab', a Persian rose water syrup. I had that fact floating around in the back of my mind, and once I combined it with the Middle Eastern custom of adding cardamom to coffee, I had the beginnings of a drink. When picking the coffee for this caffeinated cocktail, go for a dark roasted bean, full of chocolate and caramel notes. If cardamom isn't your bag, swap the Cardamom Syrup for 22ml (¾fl oz) Mint Syrup (see page 16) and skip the rose water entirely. The zing of the Mint Syrup will pair nicely with the smoke of the cold brew coffee to make the perfect summer iced coffee. (For a guide to making cold brew coffee, turn to page 55.)**

Fill a julep tin or Old Fashioned glass with ice and set aside for 5 minutes to chill or pop it in the freezer for 15–30 minutes.

Half-fill a shaker with ice and pour in the cold brew coffee, Cardamom Syrup, and rose water. Seal and shake well for 30 seconds or so to chill the mixture. Empty the ice cubes from the julep tin or glass, then add crushed ice and strain in the Coffee & Cardamom Julep. Serve straight away.

ROSSO
ROSSO
0.0%
LAGER
ALCOHOL
FREE

# Spritz di Birra

**SERVES 1**

50ml (1¾fl oz) Sanbittèr Rosso, chilled
120ml (4fl oz) alcohol-free IPA, chilled
Lemon twist, to garnish

This long, refreshing, alcohol-free beer cocktail is made with Sanbittèr Rosso, a no-alcohol Italian drink with a sweet herbal flavour that you can find in delis and speciality drink stores. It pairs brilliantly with the hoppy bitterness of a zero-proof IPA beer to make a great alternative to the standard Italian Spritzes. IPAs – aka Indian Pale Ales – are typically malty and heavy on the hops, the flowers that were used to preserve barrels of beer on long sea journeys to India (hence the name). Hops can be bitter, fruity, floral and citrusy, and different brewers emphasize the flavours they prefer. More and more alcohol-free IPAs are coming onto the market, so you can try different drinks until you find the IPA you like best. Once you've found the one you like, stir yourself a Spritz and serve it alongside plates of hams and salamis, tomato-topped bruschette and bowls of olives for an at-home aperitivo hour.

Fill a Collins glass with ice cubes and pour in the chilled Sanbittèr Rosso. Slowly top up with the IPA. Let it settle, then give it a gentle stir and drop in a lemon twist to garnish.

# La Parisienne

**SERVES 1**

1 barley tea bag
1 litre (1.7 pints) cold water
15ml (½fl oz) Gin Botanicals Syrup (see page 16)
15ml (½fl oz) fresh lemon juice
Chilled tonic water, to top up
Lemon twist, to garnish

**This fancy sparkler is made with barley tea, a nutty-tasting brew with a biscuit-cracker flavour that's not unlike the toasty notes you find in Champagne (for more about barley tea, see the notes in the box). Of course, Champagne also fizzes, so in this drink the sparkle comes from a splash of tonic water. Add a citrusy dash of Gin Botanicals Syrup (see page 16) and you end up with a crisp, savoury, effervescent, non-alcoholic cocktail. It's a foggy-coloured drink, capped with a fine layer of white foam, like mist swirling down the Seine. Take a sip and imagine walking through the streets of Paris, wrapped in a warm coat and with the cold air stinging your cheeks. When you find your favourite imagined café, with a view of the Eiffel Tower, take a seat and enjoy a glass of this fizz.**

Make the barley tea by steeping 1 barley tea bag in the cold water for 2 hours.

Strain the tea and discard the tea bag. Pour 50ml (1¾fl oz) of the tea into a shaker (you can keep the rest in the fridge for a couple of days – it's delicious cold). Add the Gin Botanicals Syrup and lemon juice. Add a handful of ice cubes, seal the shaker and shake well. Strain the mix into a flute glass and top up with chilled tonic water. Give it a quick stir and garnish with a lemon twist.

**Barley tea is good for you because...**

...it may help to keep your teeth pearly white. Popular in Japan (where it's called *mugicha*) and Korea (where it's known as *boricha*), barley tea is not actually a tea but a tisane made with roasted barley grains. You can make it by steeping the barley tea in hot water for a few minutes or cold brewing it for a few hours to make a cooling summer drink. A 2007 study found that drinks made with roasted barley may have anti-adhesive properties. Ceramic beads that had been coated with a barley beverage showed lower rates of bacterial growth than untreated beads. Swap beads for teeth and a lab for your mouth, and this could mean that drinking barley tea will protect your smile from plaque and tooth decay.

# Valentino's Kiss

**SERVES 1**

A small handful of tarragon sprigs
60ml (2fl oz) fresh orange juice
30ml (1fl oz) tart cherry juice
1 tsp apple cider vinegar
1 tsp glycerine (optional)
Orange twist, to garnish

**More than 90 years after his death, Rudolph Valentino remains the silver screen's greatest seducer. When The Sheik hit cinemas in 1921, women fainted in the aisles while men walked out in disgust, appalled at the effect this foppish actor was having on their womenfolk (whether they carried their swooning wives and girlfriends out with them, or left them to come to their senses in their own time, we can only imagine). Valentino smouldered his way through almost a dozen more movies and when I tasted this moody and seductive cocktail, I knew I had to name it after him. The drink takes an aniseed twist of tarragon and shakes it with sweet fruit juices and a sour smack of cider vinegar to make a charmingly easy-to-sip apéritif. It's a very persuasive cocktail, sexy and sophisticated. Be careful who you serve it to – you wouldn't want just anybody to fall at your feet. Would you?**

Fill a coupe glass with ice and set aside for 5 minutes to chill or pop it in the freezer for 15–30 minutes.

Place the tarragon sprigs in a shaker and use a muddler or a wooden spoon to bash them a few times to bruise them and release the aromatic oils. Pour in the orange juice, cherry juice, and cider vinegar. Add the glycerine, if you're using it, to give the drink a softer texture, and a handful of ice cubes. Seal and shake well to chill. Tip the ice out of the coupe glass, then strain in the chilled mixture. Garnish with an orange twist and serve.

# La Passeggiata

**SERVES 1**

45ml (1½fl oz) fresh ruby grapefruit juice
45ml (1½fl oz) Ginger Switchel
8ml (¼fl oz) Bitter Apéritif syrup
A dash of soda water, chilled
Grapefruit twist, to garnish

At 5pm, when the sun starts to soften in the sky and the light turns dusky, the streets in every town, city and village in Italy will begin to fill. Families step out together and walk along the streets and around the piazzas. They greet friends and stop to trade news and share gossip until around 8pm, when they head home for dinner. This is *la passeggiata*, the moment in the day when work is put aside and everybody gathers to see and be seen. In between strolling, people often stop for a drink and snack at a bar, and this spirit-free drink was inspired by the aromatic cocktails that appear on aperitivo menus. It's made with a dash of Bitter Apéritif syrup, a deep red syrup with a moreish herbal flavour that you can find in speciality liquor and coffee supply stores. Stirred with grapefruit juice, Ginger Switchel and a dash of soda, it makes a tall, frothy, pink drink that's crisp and refreshing, with just enough sour sharpness to make it interesting.

Add a large handful of ice to a shaker and pour in the grapefruit juice, Ginger Switchel and Bitter Apéritif syrup. Seal and shake well to chill. Fill a Collins glass with ice cubes and strain in the grapefruit mix. Add a dash of soda water to top up and gently stir together. Garnish with a grapefruit twist to serve.

# Cold Brew Coffee Sour

**SERVES 1**

60ml (2fl oz) cold brew coffee
30ml (1fl oz) fresh lemon juice
15ml (½fl oz) Sugar-free Syrup (see page 15)
1 tsp glycerine (optional)
15ml (½fl oz) fresh egg white or aquafaba (the liquid from a tin of chickpeas)

**Cold brew coffee is good for you because...**

...it could help boost your mood. Cold brew coffee is made by steeping coffee grounds in cold water for up to 48 hours to extract their flavour. Cold brewing should give you a less bitter cup of coffee, which is one reason to rejoice, but it may also help improve your mood. A 2011 Harvard study found that women who drink at least four cups of coffee a day had a substantially lower risk of developing depression, which is something to smile about when you pour your morning cup of joe.

The three-ingredient Sour is a cocktail classic. At its simplest it's a mix of a base drink shaken with citrus, a sweetener and ice to make a mouth-wateringly sweet-and-sour cocktail. There are an increasing number of zero-proof distilled spirits on the market that would make a great Sour – try a gin alternative with lime and Simple Syrup (see page 15), or a rum version with lemon and Demerara (Raw) Syrup (see page 16). But if you want to give Sour-making a go and only have the contents of your kitchen cupboard to play with, reach for a bag of coffee. This recipe uses cold brew coffee (turn to page 55 for a guide to cold brewing) but it would work just as well with fresh coffee – just let it cool a little and use plenty of ice to chill it quickly. I've included glycerine in the recipe, as it gives the drink a richer texture, and egg white or aquafaba to create a fine layer of foam – both are optional. Try it with and without them to find the Sour mix that suits you.

Fill a coupe glass with ice and set aside for 5 minutes to chill or pop it in the freezer for 15–30 minutes.

Half-fill a shaker with ice and pour in the cold brew coffee, lemon juice, Sugar-free Syrup and glycerine, if you're using it. Add the egg white or aquafaba. Seal and shake well for 30 seconds or so to chill the mix. Strain into a clean glass or jug (not the coupe glass), then tip the ice out of the shaker. Pour the mix back into the shaker, seal and dry shake for another 30 seconds or so to foam the egg white/aquafaba. Tip the ice out of the coupe glass, then strain in the Cold Brew Coffee Sour and serve straight away.

# La Brava

**SERVES 1**

½ tsp sea salt flakes, plus an extra pinch to season
A pinch of cayenne pepper
1 lime wedge
60ml (2fl oz) fresh lime juice
2 tsp Worcestershire sauce
2–3 tsp hot sauce, such as Cholula, Tapatío, Valentina or Tabasco®
400ml (14fl oz) alcohol-free lager, chilled

**This peppy, zero-proof version of a spicy Mexican lager cocktail is an invigorating mix of alcohol-free lager spiked with lime juice, Worcestershire sauce and a fiery splash of hot sauce. How much chilli heat you add is up to you, but don't be too shy. The drink is best when it has enough of a kick to make your mouth wake up. The drink's stimulating effect makes it a good choice for brunch, when you fancy a change from the usual tomato or orange juice-based cocktails. It's also really good for barbecues, especially when served in an ice-cold frosted glass on a blisteringly hot day.**

If you have time, place a pilsner or pint glass in the fridge or freezer to chill for up 1 hour so the glass is nice and frosty.

When you're ready to mix the drink, tip the salt and cayenne into a saucer and stir to mix. Rub half the rim of the chilled glass with the lime wedge, then dip it in the spicy salt mix to coat. Pour the lime juice, Worcestershire sauce and hot sauce into the glass (use more or less hot sauce, depending on how spicy it is and how much fire you'd like your drink to have). Add a small pinch of salt and stir to mix. Pour in the chilled alcohol-free lager to top up and serve.

HOT
SAUCE
0.0%
0.0%
LAGER
ALCOHOL
FREE

# Up All Night

**SERVES 1**

45ml (1½fl oz) Sanbittèr Rosso
45ml (1½fl oz) cold brew coffee
10ml (¼fl oz) apple cider vinegar
1 tsp glycerine (optional)
Maraschino cherry, to garnish

**Apple cider vinegar is good for you because...**

...it's thought to reduce risk factors for heart disease. Apple cider vinegar has been considered an elixir for good health for thousands of years. Hippocrates, the Ancient Greek father of modern medicine, recommended using it to clean wounds. When it comes to heart health, animal studies have shown that apple cider vinegar can help to lower cholesterol and triglyceride levels, which could reduce the risk of developing heart disease.

**This drink could easily position itself equally as the perfect libation at the end of the evening or at the start of the day. It's a smoky red drink that matches the rich, roasted aroma of cold brew coffee with the lush, bittersweet flavour of Sanbittèr Rosso, an Italian soft drink that you can find in delis and speciality drink stores. It's a very grown-up drink that reminds me of the fug of basement bars late at night, and also the cosy atmosphere of a diner at breakfast. Perhaps the best thing to do is stay up all night, then you can make yourself one of these cocktails and toast the rising of the sun.**

Fill a coupe glass with ice and set aside for 5 minutes to chill or pop it in the freezer for 15–30 minutes.

Half-fill a stirring glass with ice, then pour in the Sanbittèr Rosso, cold brew coffee, apple cider vinegar, and glycerine, if you're using it (the glycerine gives the drink a richer texture). Stir well for 1–2 minutes to chill. Tip the ice out of the coupe glass, then strain in the drink mixture. Drop in a maraschino cherry and serve.

SERVE

45ml (1
Garc
non-
disti
22ml (¾
Corc
or se
150ml (
lemo
soda
Chilled
to to
Lime w
sprig

# Doctor's Orders

**SERVES 2**

1 tsp Lapsang Souchong tea leaves
150ml (5¼fl oz) boiling water
150ml (5¼fl oz) Ginger Switchel (see page 21)
30ml (1fl oz) fresh lemon juice
2 tsp Honey Syrup (see page 17)
Lemon twists, to garnish

**Fans of smoky flavours will love this long drink, based around Lapsang Souchong tea. Originally from the mountainous Wuyi province in Fujian, China, Lapsang Souchong is a black tea that's dried over pinewood fires. The drying process gives the tea an intense, smoke-filled aroma that people either love or hate. Combined with Ginger Switchel in this warmly flavoured drink, it almost tastes leathery. A little like drinking the atmosphere of an old-fashioned library, one lined with shelves full of ancient books, with a fire crackling in the corner and a decanter of something reviving on the desk. Switchel is reputed to have many health benefits (go to page 21 to find out more), as it has the magic combination of lemon juice and honey. If you're feeling in need of a pick-me-up, stir together a glass of this restorative drink and enjoy the beneficial effects.**

Make the tea by placing the Lapsang Souchong tea leaves in a heatproof jug and pouring over the boiling water, then leave to steep for 5 minutes.

Strain the tea, discarding the tea leaves, and set aside to cool. When you're ready to make the cocktail, fill two Old Fashioned glasses with ice cubes. Divide the cooled tea between the glasses, then follow suit with the Ginger Switchel, lemon juice and Honey Syrup, dividing them equally between the glasses. Stir well to mix and chill. Drop a lemon twist into each glass and serve.

# Cat's Meow

**SERVES 1**

45ml (1½fl oz) Ginger Switchel (see page 21)
8ml (¼fl oz) Honey Syrup (see page 17)
45ml (1½fl oz) fresh orange juice
1 tsp glycerine (optional)
Lemon twist, to garnish

**A dinky drink that makes a stylish aperitif, this alcohol-free cocktail is the bee's knees, the cat's pyjamas, and the Cat's Meow. It's a lot of praise to heap on one drink, but I think it lives up to the hype – especially if you like ginger biscuits or cookies. The mix of Ginger Switchel with fresh orange juice and Honey Syrup creates a liquid gingerbread effect, one that's cosily chic – like chunky knit sweaters or cashmere socks. Throughout the book I've made glycerine optional because not everyone will want the slightly thicker, softer texture it gives to drinks (for more about glycerine, turn to page 12). But in small coupe cocktails that are served up, like this one, I think it does add an extra element that really benefits the drink.**

Fill a small coupe glass with ice and set aside for 5 minutes to chill or pop it in the freezer for 15–30 minutes.

Half-fill a shaker with ice and pour in the Ginger Switchel, Honey Syrup, orange juice and glycerine, if you're using it. Seal and shake well for 30 seconds or so to chill the mixture. Tip the ice out of the coupe glass then strain in the drink, drop in a lemon twist and serve.

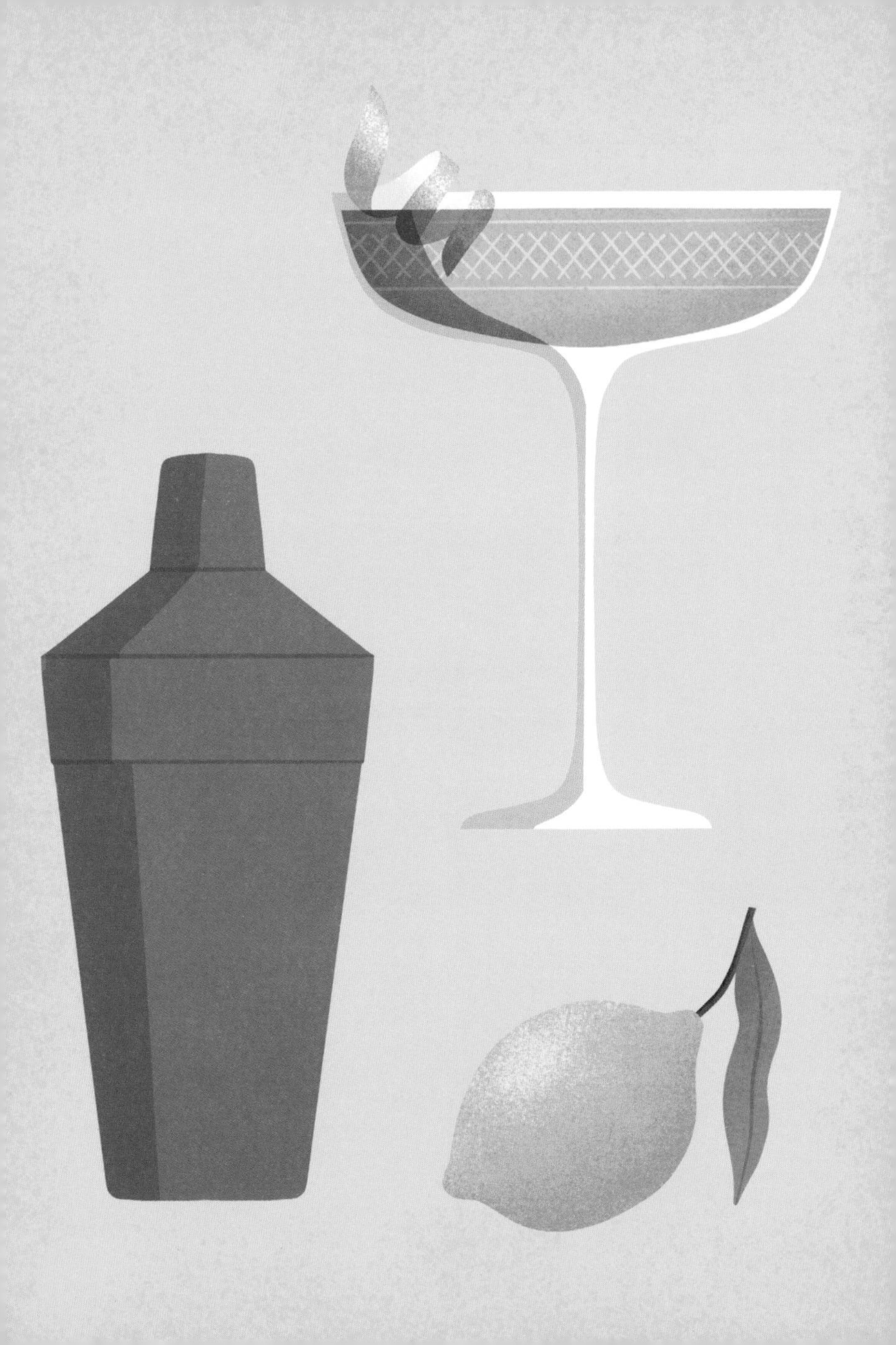

# Kiss Me Quick

**SERVES 1**

45ml (1½fl oz) fresh grapefruit juice
45ml (1½fl oz) cranberry juice drink
45ml (1½fl oz) peach nectar
15ml (½fl oz) grenadine
½ tsp orange flower water
1 tsp glycerine (optional)
Orange slice, to garnish

A lot of things were big in the 80s; backcombed hair, shoulder pads, legwarmers and neon-coloured fruit-based drinks all loomed large – sometimes literally. This bubblegum-pink, spirit-free cocktail is a throwback to all those fruity Martinis and brightly hued jugs of drinks that cheered up bars and parties during the Yuppie Years. It's a heady mix of fruit juices souped up by the addition of grenadine, a concentrated syrup made from pomegranate juice that has a zippy, mouthwatering flavour (see page 12 for more about grenadine). A dash of orange flower water gives the drink a perfume hit (be careful when you're measuring the orange flower water – it's very potent and drinks can go from floral to soapy if you add too much). It's tart, tasty and a little bit cheeky – a drink for retro fans who want an excuse to get their power suits back out and party like it's 1985.

Fill a large coupe glass with ice and set aside for 5 minutes to chill or pop it in the freezer for 15–30 minutes.

Half-fill a shaker with ice and pour in all the fruit juices, the peach nectar, grenadine, orange flower water, and glycerine, if you're using it (the glycerine adds texture). Seal and shake well for 30 seconds or so to chill the fruity mixture. Tip the ice out of the coupe glass, then strain in the drink. Garnish with an orange slice to serve.

# Blackberry & Ginger Cooler

**SERVES 1**

45ml (1½fl oz) apple juice
75ml (2½fl oz) Ginger Switchel (see page 21)
15ml (½fl oz) fresh lemon juice
45ml (1½oz) Blackberry & Bay Cordial (see page 20)
Blackberries, to garnish

**Going foraging for blackberries is an end-of-summer tradition in my house. When I was a kid I'd go blackberrying with my friends. We'd cycle to the park, plastic tubs and bags ready, then work our way along the bramble bushes that lined the fields and fences. No matter how many we picked (or ate), there always seemed to be more blackberries when we went back. For a few weeks in August and September, there would always be a blackberry and apple pie on Sunday. I still keep a look out for blackberry bushes now and when I've found a good patch, I watch the berries grow and race to pick them as soon as they're hanging heavy on the branches, deep purple and full of juice. I can't eat all the blackberries I pick these days, so turning them into a cordial is one way to preserve their lush flavour. There's a recipe for Blackberry & Bay Cordial on page 20, which pairs beautifully with Ginger Switchel (see page 21) in this drink to make a long, cooling cocktail that has a pungent mix of sugar and spice.**

Half-fill a shaker with ice and add the apple juice, Ginger Switchel, lemon juice and Blackberry & Bay Cordial. Seal and shake well for 30 seconds or so to chill. Fill a Collins glass with crushed ice and pour in the apple and blackberry mix. Stir to mix, then drop in a couple of blackberries to serve.

# Garden Spritz

**SERVES 1**

1 Earl Grey tea bag or 2 tsp Earl Grey tea leaves
Boiling water, to brew the tea
15ml (½fl oz) fresh lemon juice
15ml (½fl oz) Lavender Syrup (see page 16)
Chilled sparkling water, to top up
Lemon slice, to garnish

**Capturing the essence of an English country garden in a drink is a deliciously romantic challenge. The words conjure up a whitewashed cottage surrounded by fragrant flowers in bloom, bumble bees buzzing between them, a rambling rose or a headily scented wisteria creeping up the walls, and shady trees offering a welcome respite from the hot summer sun. There is an obvious place to start: a cup of tea. Iced teas haven't taken off in England in the way they have in America, but I think that they make a great basis for a tall summer drink. Earl Grey, the black tea leaves brightened by bergamot oil and orange zest, has a rich botanical flavour that pairs brilliantly with lavender syrup. Together – with a splash of zingy fresh lemon juice – they evoke the green leaf and perfumed petal atmosphere of a garden hidden deep in the English countryside.**

Make the tea by adding a tea bag or 2 teaspoons of tea leaves to a mug and pour over the boiling water. Leave to steep for 4–5 minutes, then strain out the tea bag or leaves and let the tea cool a little.

When you're ready to make the cocktail, fill a Collins glass with ice cubes. Measure out 50ml (1¾fl oz) of the Earl Grey tea and add it to the glass. Pour in the lemon juice and Lavender Syrup and gently stir to mix, then top up with chilled sparkling water. Stir a few more times to just mix it all together. Drop in a slice of lemon to garnish.

# Frozen Mango & Lime Margarita

**SERVES 2**

1 mango, weighing around 600g (21oz)
30ml (1fl oz) fresh lime juice
50ml (1¾fl oz) Cardamom Syrup (see page 16)
75ml (2½fl oz) tequila alternative or similar non-alcoholic spirit
2 lime wedges, to garnish

**Mangoes are good for you because...**

...they're believed to help protect your eyesight. Mangoes are full of antioxidants, the molecules that fight free radicals in your body (the compounds that can cause harm). Two of the antioxidants found in mangoes are lutein and zeaxanthin, and these typically accumulate in your retinas. While they're there they act as a natural sunblock, absorbing excess sunlight. So, for sun-safe eyes, keep eating mangoes and definitely keep wearing sunglasses.

**Over the past couple of years there has been an explosion in the zero-proof distilled spirits market. These alternatives – or 'alts' – are made by distilling non-alcoholic spirits with herbs and spices to create the same flavour profile you find in hard liquors, but without the booze. Seedlip kicked off the process in the UK with an alcohol-free gin, and since then more companies have developed their own non-alcoholic spirits. In America, Ritual created a zero-proof tequila, which has a bright blue agave aroma mellowed with spices and charred oak. It's perfect in a spirit-free Margarita, especially when blended with tropical fresh mango and Cardamom Syrup (see page 16). If you can't find a tequila 'alt' in your local bottle shop, explore the other alcohol-free options. A zero-proof rum alternative, botanical-rich gin 'alt', or even a hoppy, citrusy non-alcoholic IPA would all make a tasty addition to this luscious iced cocktail.**

Put two margarita or large wine glasses into the freezer for 15–30 minutes to chill.

Peel the mango, then slice the flesh off the stone. You should have around 400g (14oz) mango flesh. Scoop it into a blender. Add the lime juice, Cardamom Syrup, tequila alternative or other non-alcoholic spirit and a cup of crushed ice. Blitz until smooth. Pour into the chilled glasses and garnish with a lime wedge each to serve.

# Give A Fig

**SERVES 1**

For the fig purée:
**150g (5oz) ripe figs**
**2 tbsp cold water**

For the cocktail:
**22ml (¾fl oz) Basil Syrup (see page 16)**
**15ml (½fl oz) fresh lemon juice**
**Chilled sparkling water, to top up**
**Basil sprig and fig half, to garnish**

**Velvety-skinned figs are one of my favourite treats. The first sighting of a box of plump figs in the greengrocers, each one carefully wrapped in paper, is always exciting and also painfully expensive. As the fig season progresses (and they get mercifully cheaper) I fill my fridge with these fruits, and their intoxicating scent perfumes the kitchen. Figs pair beautifully with so many flavours. For this drink I've gone with basil. The king of summer herbs, preserved in a Simple Syrup (see page 15), has a pungent green aroma with a hint of liquorice that marries well with the fig's earthy sweetness. For me, this drink tastes like a stroll in the Tuscan countryside at the end of summer. The warm Italian sunshine that ripened the figs and fed the basil leaves is captured in the cocktail's gentle fizz, making it the perfect drink to serve on the final night of a holiday – even if you haven't gone any further than your own backyard.**

Make the fig purée by trimming the woody ends off the figs, then roughly chop the figs and pop them into a bowl. Add the cold water and use a hand-held blender to blitz until they're smooth – if it seems too thick, add another tablespoon of water. The fig purée will keep in the fridge for 1–2 days in a sealed tub.

To make the cocktail, fill an Old Fashioned glass with ice cubes and pour in 50ml (1¾fl oz) of the fig purée. Add the Basil Syrup and lemon juice and top up with sparkling water. Gently stir to mix. Tuck in a basil sprig and place half a fig in the glass to garnish. Serve straight away.

# Blueberry & Mint Mojito

**SERVES 1**

15g (½oz) blueberries
2 mint sprigs, plus extra to garnish
1 lime wedge
45ml (1½fl oz) Blueberry & Mint Cordial (see page 20)
22ml (¾fl oz) fresh lime juice
Chilled soda water, to top up

**Blueberries are good for you because...**

...they are high in antioxidants. One of the first foods to be dubbed a 'superfood', blueberries have one of the highest levels of antioxidants found in commonly eaten foods. Antioxidants are compounds that protect your body from the damaging effects of free radicals, the molecules that may contribute to diseases, such as cancer, and ageing. So maybe instead of an apple a day to keep the doctor away, go for a handful of blueberries instead.

**On the Yorkshire Moors, in the North of England, you'll find bushes of bilberries growing amid the heather. These small blue berries have an acidic flavour, so they're normally cooked with sugar and mint and turned into pies known locally as mucky mouth pies – so-called because enthusiastic eaters of bilberry pies often end up with blue mouths, tongues and chins. You shouldn't end up with a blue face when you drink this Blueberry & Mint Mojito, although I guess that's down to how you drink it. It's made with the more easily available blueberries, although if you do manage to get hold of bilberries (also called huckleberries, blaeberries, whortleberries and winberries), feel free to swap them in. To give the drink an extra shot of berry sweetness, I've added Blueberry & Mint Cordial to the mix of fresh blueberries, mint and lime – you'll find the recipe on page 20.**

Place the blueberries, mint sprigs, and lime wedge in a Collins glass and use a muddler or the end of a wooden spoon to crush them together. Pour in the Blueberry & Mint Cordial and the lime juice and stir together. Add a handful of ice cubes then pour in enough soda water to top up the glass. Give everything a gentle stir just to mix it together. Tuck in a fresh mint sprig or two and serve with reusable straws if liked.

KOMBUCHA

# Hot Ginger Fizz

**SERVES 1**

15ml (½fl oz) fresh lime juice
8ml (¼fl oz) Ginger Syrup (see page 16)
75ml (2½fl oz) ginger kombucha
Chilled soda water, to top up
Lime wedge, to garnish

**Kombucha is good for you because...**

...it is thought to do your gut some good. Kombucha is made by fermenting sweetened tea with a SCOBY ('symbiotic culture of bacteria and yeasts'). The SCOBY converts the sugar into ethanol and then acetic acid, which is why kombucha has a tangy flavour. Along the way it produces probiotic bacteria. These are the friendly kind that can help keep your gut microbiome in balance. The jury is still out on just how much kombucha helps your digestive system, but it is definitely delicious as a drink.

This cocktail comes with a double hit of ginger. There's a dash of fiery Ginger Syrup (see page 16) and a good slug of ginger kombucha, the fermented tea drink that started popping up in Western health food stores in the early 2000s and continues to grow and grow in popularity (for more about kombucha, see the box below). This drink offers a nice warming kick with every sip. Before you top up the drink with soda water, taste it. If you like the mix of ginger and citrus as it is, just pour in a splash more ginger kombucha to fill up the glass. For something a bit more restrained, add a dash of soda. It's worth noting that kombuchas typically contain a small amount of alcohol (usually less than 0.5% ABV), so if you do want a completely zero-proof drink, swap the ginger kombucha for alcohol-free ginger beer.

Fill a copper mug or highball glass with ice cubes. Pour in the lime juice, Ginger Syrup and ginger kombucha. Gently stir for 30 seconds or so to chill, then top up with a dash or two of chilled soda water. Stir a few more times to just mix it all together. Drop in a lime wedge to garnish and serve with reusable straws.

# Buck's Twist

**SERVES 1**

45ml (1½fl oz) apple juice
35ml (1¼fl oz) fresh orange juice
60ml (2fl oz) Ginger Switchel (see page 21)
½ tsp orange flower water
1 tsp glycerine (optional)
Orange twist, to garnish

The Buck's Club is a gentlemen's club located in London. It was opened in 1919 by Captain H. J. Buckmaster, who gave the club its name and fitted it out with an American Bar where at least two famous orange-based cocktails were invented – the Buck's Fizz and the Sidecar. So it seemed appropriate to name this citrusy, booze-free cocktail after Buck's. It's a mellow mix of orange and apple juice with a lingering dash of ginger heat that will warm you up from the inside out. With an autumnal feel, it's the kind of drink to shake up after a brisk walk on a frosty afternoon, then sip in front of a cosy fire. The recipe includes glycerine, which gives the drink a slightly viscous texture. If you'd prefer your drink to be sharper and brighter, leave out the glycerine.

Fill a small coupe glass with ice and set aside for 5 minutes to chill or pop it in the freezer for 15–30 minutes.

Half-fill a shaker with ice and pour in the apple and orange juices. Add the Ginger Switchel, orange flower water and glycerine, if you're using it. Seal and shake well to chill. Tip the ice out of the coupe glass, then strain in the mixture. Garnish with an orange twist and serve.

# Hot Buttered Apple Juice

**SERVES 4–6**

For the spiced butter:
125g (4oz) lightly salted butter, softened
110g (3¾oz) Demerara sugar
½ tsp ground cinnamon
½ tsp allspice
¼ tsp ground cloves
A good grating of nutmeg

To serve:
750ml (1.3 pints) cloudy or freshly pressed apple juice
30ml (1fl oz) fresh lemon juice
Grated nutmeg, to garnish

**Adding a spoonful of spiced butter to a hot drink instantly creates a snug, festive atmosphere. It's the mix of spices – the cinnamon, allspice and cloves – that smell like a Christmas party, while the butter gives any drink a silky texture. For this winter warmer I've used a gingerbread-spiced butter to enrich a gently simmering pan of apple juice. Use a good-quality cloudy apple juice or freshly pressed apple juice for the best results and add all the butter to the pan only if you're serving the Hot Buttered Apple Juice straight away. If you're serving it individually over the course of a party, measure out 2 tablespoons of butter into a glass when you're ready to serve and pour in around 100–150ml (3½–5¼fl oz) warm apple juice. Stir to blend together, then grate over the nutmeg.**

To make the spiced butter, scoop the softened butter into a bowl and add the Demerara sugar. Beat together with electric beaters until smoothly combined. Add all the spices and beat again. Scoop into a tub, seal and store in the fridge. The butter will keep in the fridge for up to 4 weeks.

To make the Hot Buttered Apple Juice, pour the apple and lemon juices into a pan on a medium heat. Cover with a lid and gently warm for 5–6 minutes until steaming hot. Scoop the spiced butter into the pan and stir until dissolved (see above for instructions if you are not serving all at once). Ladle the buttered apple juice into mugs or heatproof glasses and grate over a little extra nutmeg to serve.

# Carrot Colada

**SERVES 1**

35ml (1¼fl oz) carrot juice
35ml (1¼fl oz) fresh clementine juice
45ml (1½fl oz) coconut milk kefir
15ml (½fl oz) fresh lemon juice
10ml (¼fl oz) Five-spice Syrup (see page 16)
Clementine slice, to garnish

**What do you get when you cross a carrot cake with a Piña Colada? This tasty dessert in a glass. Less messy than putting an actual slice of carrot cake through a juicer, this creamy drink gets its sweet and spicy flavour from a dash of Five-spice Syrup (see page 16). The combination of fennel, star anise, cinnamon, cloves and Sichuan peppercorns blends beautifully with a mix of carrot and clementine juices, while coconut milk kefir stands in for the cream cheese frosting. If you want to make it for a party, multiply the ingredients by the number of guests and whizz together in a blender with a cupful of crushed ice before serving.**

Half-fill a shaker with ice, then pour in the carrot and clementine juices, the coconut milk kefir, lemon juice and the Five-spice Syrup. Seal and shake well to chill. Fill a tumbler or Old Fashioned glass with ice cubes, then strain in the Carrot Colada. Garnish with a slice of clementine and serve straight away.

# Frozen Lychee Martini

**SERVES 1**

6 lychees, fresh or from a can
45ml (1½fl oz) Seedlip Spice 94 or similar non-alcoholic distilled spirit
8ml (¼fl oz) fresh lime juice
Lime twist, to garnish

A mini snow cone of a cocktail, this iced drink gets its smooth texture and sweet rose-and-pear flavour from a generous handful of lychees. The Queen of Fruits in China, lychees – or *litchis* – are delicately perfumed and best eaten soon after they are picked, which is why canned lychees are such a feature on supermarket shelves. Getting ripe lychees to market while they're still lusciously aromatic is a race against time, so canned lychees are a handy and reliable standby. I've paired them with a gin alternative that has a warm, spicy flavour. If you can't find it in your local drinks store, look out for other zero-proof distilled spirits. If gin botanicals aren't for you, try a tequila alternative instead. The herbaceous blue agave notes will work well with the lychees' floral aroma.

Fill a small coupe glass or martini glass with ice and set aside for 5 minutes to chill or pop it in the freezer for 15–30 minutes.

Peel and stone the lychees if they're fresh, or scoop them out of the tin and shake off any excess syrup. Add them to a blender with the Seedlip Spice 94 or other gin alternative, the lime juice and half a cup of crushed ice. Blitz until smooth then pour into the chilled coupe glass. Garnish with a lime twist and serve.

# Mocha Mockatini

**SERVES 1**

35ml (1¼floz) fresh espresso
22ml (¾fl oz) Chocolate Syrup (see page 17)
45ml (1½fl oz) double cream
Chocolate for grating, to serve

**Sitting somewhere between a chocolate mousse and an Espresso Martini, this spectacular dessert drink is a real treat. It has a silky texture and a malted, brown-sugar lick of astringency, thanks to the coffee. The flavour reminds me of coffee creams, the bittersweet fondants coated in chocolate that used to appear at Christmas, as part of a tin of festive chocolates. They were the perfect mix of milky sweetness and tart coffee beans. Served in elegant coupe glasses with buttery shortbread on the side, this Mockatini would make a stylish end to a meal.**

Fill a small coupe glass with ice and set aside for 5 minutes to chill or pop it in the freezer for 15–30 minutes.

Half-fill a shaker with ice and pour in the espresso, Chocolate Syrup and double cream. Seal and shake well for 30 seconds or so to chill the drink. Tip the ice out of the glass, then strain in the cocktail. Grate over a little chocolate to serve.

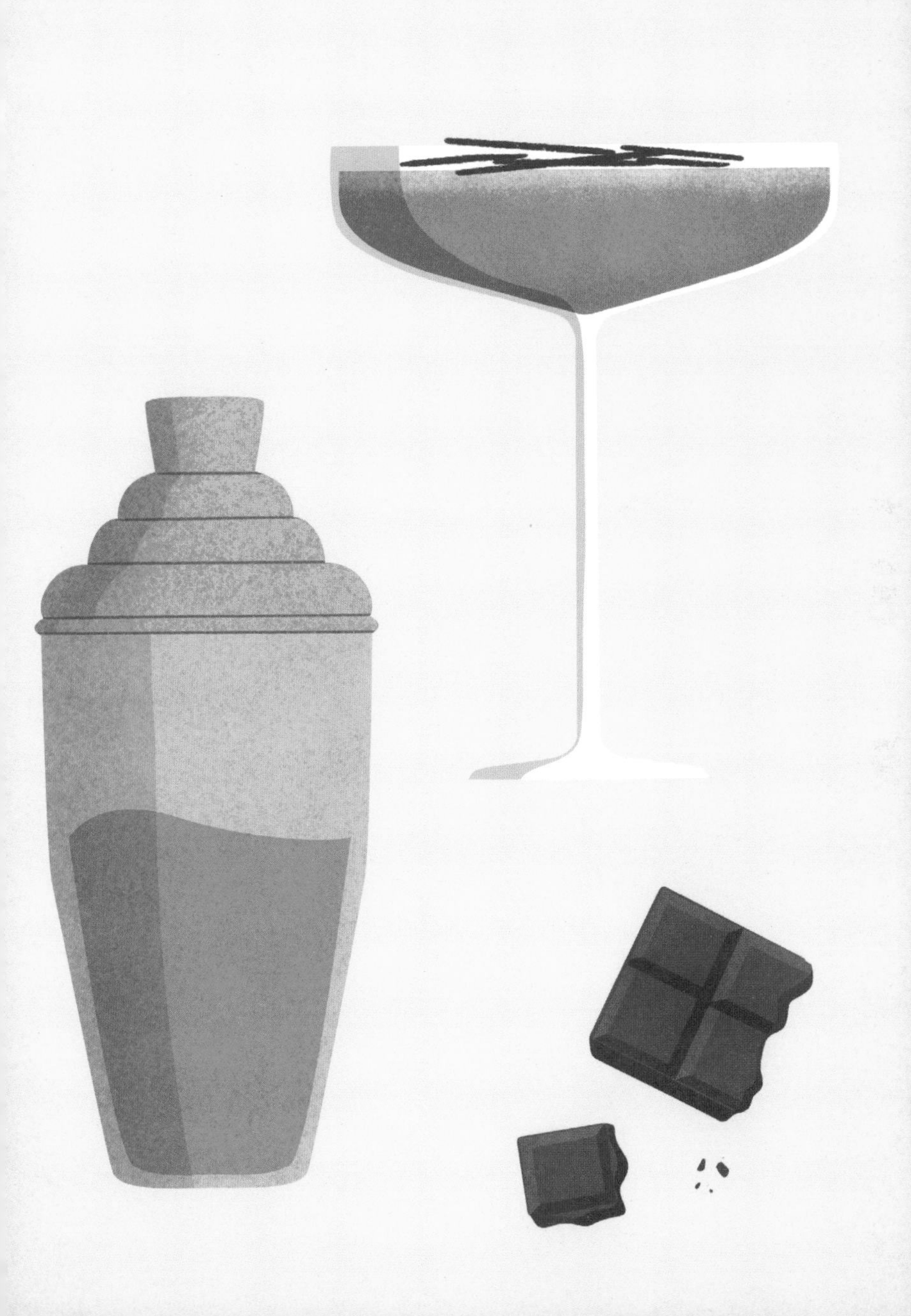

# Apple Mockatini

**SERVES 1**

45ml (1½fl oz) apple juice
22ml (¾fl oz) fresh lemon juice
15ml (½fl oz) Demerara (Raw) Syrup (see page 17)
1 tsp glycerine (optional)
Apple slices, to garnish

**The all-American apple pie was the inspiration for this alcohol-free cocktail, which is heavy on the apple but brightened up by a dash of lemon juice and sweetened with the rich, rounded flavour of Demerara (Raw) Syrup. Use a good-quality pressed apple juice when you're making this cocktail – it's the centrepiece of the show, so it's worth buying the best juice you can (or juicing apples yourself, if you're very keen). This version is a straightforward, apple-heavy drink. If you want to add some American diner vibes, add 3–4 cinnamon sticks to the Demerara (Raw) Syrup when you're making it (see page 17 for the recipe). Alternatively, add ½ teaspoon vanilla extract to the shaker with the other ingredients for a drink that is a bit more like the apple pie Mom used to make. It's a great cocktail to serve at the end of dinner, especially with bowls of vanilla ice cream and wafer biscuits.**

Fill a small coupe glass with ice and set aside for 5 minutes to chill or pop it in the freezer for 15–30 minutes.

Half-fill a shaker with ice and pour in the apple juice, lemon juice, Demerara (Raw) Syrup and glycerine, if you're using it (the glycerine adds texture and smoothness to the drink). Seal and shake well for 30 seconds or so to chill the mixture. Tip the ice out of the coupe glass, then strain in the Mockatini. Drop in a couple of apple slices and serve.

# Fire & Ice

**SERVES 1**

A scoop of mango sorbet
22ml (¾fl oz) Ginger Syrup (see page 16)
150ml (5¼fl oz) tonic water, chilled
Red chilli, cut in half, to garnish

A couple of years ago I heard a radio interview with Zoe Laughlin, an artist who'd investigated the flavour impact of cutlery. She led a group of volunteers who tasted forks and spoons made from different metals, then tried to work out the best metal and food pairings. They hit on a few great combinations but the one everybody loved was mango sorbet eaten off a gold spoon. Tasters described the blending of lush mango sorbet with gold as 'just heaven'. So if you have any solid-gold goblets locked away in your drinks cabinet, dust them off and use them to serve this cocktail. Half dessert, half drink, it's a stylish riff on the Coke Float. The Ginger Syrup adds a warming splash of heat, mirrored by the chilli garnish. It's a great cooler for sunny days.

Pop a scoop of mango sorbet into a large wine glass or copa glass. Drizzle over the Ginger Syrup, then pour in the chilled tonic water. Drop a chilli half into the glass and serve.

# Cucumber & Jalapeño Margarita

**SERVES 2**

½ tsp sea salt flakes
½ tsp caster sugar
A pinch of cayenne pepper
1 lime wedge
200g (7oz) cucumber
1 green jalapeño chilli
75ml (2½fl oz) cold water
30ml (1fl oz) fresh orange juice
30ml (1fl oz) fresh lime juice
15ml (½fl oz) agave syrup
8ml (¼fl oz) unsweetened pickled gherkin brine
2 lime twists, to garnish

There's green, green, and more green in this spicy but soothing riff on a Frozen Margarita. Cucumbers are famous for their cooling properties, and teaming them with a jalapeño chilli makes for an interesting mix of refreshing, grassy-hued hydration with a lip-tingling trace of heat (if you're not keen on spice, simply slice out the seeds and you'll get the fruity flavour of the chilli pepper without the fire). A spoonful of brine scooped straight from the pickle jar adds a vinegary tang to the drink, while a mix of citrus juices brighten the flavours. One of my guinea pigs tried this Marg and immediately said: 'This would make a lovely sorbet.' If you'd like to try turning this Margarita into an iced dessert, double the quantities but swap the water for 150ml (5¼fl oz) Simple Syrup. Churn in an ice-cream maker until smooth, then freeze, or pour into a tub and freeze, stirring with a fork every few hours, until you have a crunchy granita. Serve a scoop on top of a summery tomato salad.

Tip the salt, sugar, and cayenne into a saucer. Rub half the rim of two margarita or large wine glasses with a lime wedge, then dip it in the salt and sugar mix to coat. Set aside in the fridge. Roughly chop the cucumber and pop it in a blender. Trim the chilli and roughly chop it (for less heat, scoop out the seeds). Add to the blender. Pour in the water, orange and lime juices, agave syrup and pickle brine and add a cup of crushed ice. Blitz until smooth. Taste and add a little more lime juice or agave syrup if you think it needs it. Pour into the margarita or wine glasses and garnish with a lime twist to serve.

**Cucumbers are good for you because...**

...they help keep you hydrated. We all know we should drink six to eight glasses of water every day, but some people get up to 40% of their total water intake from food. This is where cucumbers come in. They are up to 95% water, which makes them a helpfully hydrating vegetable. Eating plenty of fruit and veg, like cucumbers, can help you meet your daily fluid needs, even if you miss drinking a glass or two of the good stuff (aka water).

# Jarra de Verano

**SERVES 6–8**

2 English breakfast tea bags or 2 tbsp loose English breakfast tea
350ml (12fl oz) boiling water
350ml (12fl oz) tart cherry juice
250ml (8½fl oz) orange juice
250ml (8½fl oz) sparkling water, chilled
Orange, lemon and lime slices, to serve

**Tart cherry juice is good for you because...**

...it can help reduce muscle soreness. You'll find plenty of anthocyanins in tart cherry juice and these antioxidants have powerful anti-inflammatory properties, helping to reduce swelling in tired muscles after exercise. Studies have found that drinking tart cherry juice in the run up to events like marathons or cycling competitions helps minimize post-event aches and pains.

**A jug of Sangria on a sunny day is a summer must-have, but how to recreate that Spanish holiday feeling without the alcohol? Finding a booze-free replacement for wine is tricky. Non-alcoholic wines are hit and miss, and often quite sweet. Grape juice is too one-note. To recreate Sangria without the wine, I needed a full-bodied soft drink with plenty of heft and bite. The solution was English breakfast tea. A robust blend of Assam, Ceylon and Kenyan teas, English breakfast tea is a chunky brew designed to kickstart the day. Left to steep for 20 minutes, not only is it strongly flavoured, it's also bitter with tannins – the compounds that give wine its astringency. Combining a thickly brewed breakfast tea with tart cherry juice results in a plummy drink that's a good approximation of a fruity red wine and great for mixing with orange juice and sparkling water to create a sober Spanish summer drink.**

Make the tea by pouring the boiling water over the tea bags or tea leaves in a heatproof jug, then leave to steep for 20 minutes so it's good and strong. Strain out the tea bags or leaves, then let the tea cool.

Half-fill a large jug with ice and pour in the cooled tea along with the cherry and orange juices. Give it a gentle stir for 1 minute or so to mix and chill, then top up with sparkling water and gently stir again. Add slices of orange, lemon and lime to the jug and serve the Jarra de Verano in tumblers with extra ice.

# Damask Fizz

**SERVES 4**

150g (5oz) strawberries
125ml (4fl oz) Rhubarb Shrub (see page 18)
15ml (½fl oz) Cardamom Syrup (see page 16)
8ml (¼fl oz) rose water
Chilled soda water, to top up
Sliced strawberries, to garnish

**Strawberries are good for you because...**

...they're a good source of vitamin C. Also known as ascorbic acid, vitamin C helps keep cells healthy; maintains skin, bones, blood vessels, and cartilage; and it can help with wound healing. One fruit that's fit for the first aid box.

**This is one of the most romantic drinks in the book. It's a deep blush pink and tastes like a rose garden in summer, full of perfume and spice. It does, however, serve four, which must make it the first Valentine's Day-friendly mocktail suitable for a polycule. This drink was inspired by the rose sherbets – or *sharbat* – that have been prepared in Turkey since the Middle Ages. If you have a rose bush and would like to make a rose sherbert, the simplest way is to crush edible, unsprayed rose petals with sugar, then mix them with lemon juice and water and chill for a few hours until the delicate flavour of the rose has infused the liquid. Damask roses are especially prized for their sweet fragrance, and they're often used to make rose water as well as sherbet. So, for those of us who don't have a rose garden to graze on, rose water is the perfect shortcut and it gives this drink its aromatic flavour.**

Hull the strawberries and tip them into a small blender or food processor. Add the Rhubarb Shrub, Cardamom Syrup, and rose water. Blitz until smooth and combined. Pour the strawberry mix through a fine-mesh sieve into a jug, pressing the pulp to extract all the juice. Fill four Collins glasses with crushed ice and pour the strawberry mix into the glasses. Top up with a splash of chilled soda water and stir to mix with a bar spoon. Pop a few strawberry slices on top of each glass to serve.

# Happy Like Harry

**SERVES 6**

For the peach purée:
**200g (7oz) ripe peaches**
**Boiling water, to cover**
**2 tbsp caster sugar**
**100ml (3½fl oz) water**
**30ml (1fl oz) fresh lemon juice**

To assemble:
**750ml (1.3 pints) sparkling apple juice, chilled**

**Non-alcoholic drinks at parties, like weddings, can sometimes be a bit boring. More often than not it's a choice between orange juice or sparkling water, which are thirst-quenching but not very celebratory. So, if you're planning a get-together and want something chic but booze-free to hand round your guests, try this Bellini-inspired sparkler. It's made with fresh peach purée. If you'd like to cheat, buy a can of peaches in fruit juice and blitz them in your blender until they're smooth and pourable. Sparkling apple juice stands in for prosecco. To stop the drink being too sweet, make sure you add the lemon juice to the peaches – it brightens the flavours and sharpens the whole drink up.**

Pop the peaches in a heatproof bowl and pour over enough boiling water to cover them. Set aside for 5 minutes, then drain the peaches and pull off the skins – the skins should just slip off. Roughly chop the peaches, discarding the stones. Pop the peaches in a small pan with the sugar and the water. Cover the pan with a lid, set on a medium heat and bring to a gentle boil. Turn the heat down and simmer for 3–5 minutes until the peaches are soft and collapsing. Let the peaches cool for a few minutes, then add the lemon juice and blitz the peaches with their syrup in a blender or use a stick blender to blitz them in the pan. You should get a pourable peach purée. If it is too thick, add a splash more water to thin it out. Store in a tub in the fridge until you're ready to make the mocktails – it'll keep for a few days.

To make the drinks, pour 45ml (1½fl oz) peach purée into each flute glass, then top up each with 125ml (4fl oz) sparkling apple juice. Gently stir and serve.

# Watermelon, Basil & Lime Agua Fresca

**SERVES 6–8**

1kg (35oz) watermelon, chilled
1 litre (1.7 pints) ice-cold water
100–120ml (3½–4fl oz) Basil Syrup (see page 16)
45ml (1½fl oz) fresh lime juice
Basil sprigs, to garnish

**Watermelons are good for you because...**

...they're a good source of lycopene, which is thought to be good for your heart health. Lycopene is the compound that gives fruit and vegetables their red colour, and watermelon is bursting with it. Lycopene is considered to have the ability to reduce LDL cholesterol (the 'furry artery' kind) as well as lower blood pressure. A good excuse to load up your plate (and glass) with more of the red stuff.

**One of the best ways to beat the heat in Mexico is with an agua fresca. You can see jars of these brightly coloured waters lined up on market stalls across the country, ready to offer instant refreshment to passers-by. They're often flavoured with fresh seasonal fruit, as well as hibiscus flowers (*agua de Jamaica*), tamarind (*agua de tamarindo*), and rice (*agua de horchata*). This version is made with two of my favourite summer flavours – watermelon and basil. Watermelons are almost a drink in themselves, being around 92% water. Their thirst-quenching sweetness blends well with basil's intense perfume, and a sharp spritz of lime heightens all the flavours. This drink is best served ice-cold, so – if you can – chill the ingredients before you make it, or leave it for a few hours in the fridge before serving.**

Slice the skin off the watermelon, then roughly chop the flesh. You can use the tip of your knife to flick out the black pips. This is a bit time-consuming and the pips will be ground down in the blender, so it isn't essential, although it can be satisfying to do if you have the time. When the watermelon is chopped, tip it into a large blender. Add 300ml (10fl oz) of the ice-cold water, 100ml (3½fl oz) of the Basil Syrup and the lime juice and blitz until smooth. You will need a big blender to do this. If yours isn't industrial in scale, do this in two batches. Pour the blended watermelon into a jug. Stir in the remaining cold water. Taste and add more Basil Syrup if you'd like it to be sweeter. Serve in tumblers with ice cubes, if liked, and garnished with basil sprigs.

The agua fresca will keep in a covered jug in the fridge for a day or two. The fruit pulp and liquid will separate, so stir them back together before serving.

# Virgin Queen

**SERVES 6–8**

1.2kg (42oz) ripe tomatoes
250g (8½oz) cucumber
125g (4oz) celery stalks
1 jalapeño chilli
450ml (16fl oz) cold water
1 tbsp glycerine (optional)
15ml (½fl oz) fresh lemon juice
A good pinch of sea salt
A few dashes of hot sauce, such as Tabasco® (optional)
Cherry tomatoes on cocktail sticks, to garnish

**This drink is like a magic trick. In the glass it looks like water – there may be a hint of blush pink, or a dash of colour from the hot sauce, but otherwise it's as crystal clear as an Alpine lake. Yet it tastes just like ripe red tomatoes. The secret is blitzing the tomatoes into a pulp then letting them drip through a muslin cloth overnight. The tomatoes' herbaceous flavour is carried in the clear liquid that drips down into the bowl, while the colour stays with the pulp in the sieve. It's a fun drink to serve at a brunch or to pack into a flask for a picnic. Hand round glasses and ask people to guess what the main ingredient is. It normally takes a moment or two for people to realize that it's tomato – the mismatch between the colour and the flavour makes it hard to guess. It's a fresh-tasting drink, lighter than standard tomato-juice-based drinks, and with a hit of heat from the chilli and hot sauce. If Queen Mary I had the standard Bloody Mary named after her, then this zero-proof cocktail is named for her sister, Elizabeth I, the Virgin Queen.**

Roughly chop the tomatoes, cucumber, celery, and chilli. Scoop half of the chopped veg into a large blender and add half of the cold water. Blitz until smooth and combined, then pour into a jug. Repeat with the remaining veg and water (if you have a really big blender, you can blitz them all together at the same time).

Line a large colander with muslin and set it over a large bowl. Pour the tomato mix into the colander and leave it to slowly drip through overnight. In the morning you should have a colander full of dry vegetable pulp – you can discard this. The liquid in the bowl should be clear. If it is a little misty, pour it through a fine-mesh sieve lined with muslin to catch any pulp that has slipped through. Chill until you're ready to serve it. It will keep in the fridge for a day or two in a sealed jug or tub.

To serve, fill a jug with ice and pour in the tomato water. Add the glycerine, if you're using it – it gives the drink a slightly thicker texture and also a little sweetness, so I recommend you do use it in this cocktail. Then add the lemon juice, a good pinch of salt, and a few dashes of hot sauce, if you like. Stir well to mix. Taste and add a pinch more salt or a splash more hot sauce if you think it needs it. Serve in tumblers over ice with cherry tomatoes on a cocktail stick to garnish.

# Midsummer Punch

**SERVES 6–8**

25g (1oz) dried hibiscus flowers
1 litre (1.7 pints) boiling water
30ml (1fl oz) best-quality balsamic vinegar
1 tsp orange flower water
Sliced fruit, such as apples, oranges, raspberries, and strawberries, and/ or sliced cucumber and fresh mint sprigs
250ml (8½flfl oz) ginger beer, chilled

**Hibiscus tea is good for you because...**

...it may improve the health of your liver. A 2015 study treated obese hamsters with hibiscus extract and, after 10 weeks, the markers of liver damage had decreased. In 2011, another study followed overweight humans who were given a hibiscus extract; after 12 weeks the participants showed improved liver steatosis, aka fatty liver. BMI, body fat and waist-to-hip ratio also improved. These studies used an extract rather than the tea, but happily the tea is delicious whether or not it improves your liver.

The summer solstice falls in mid-June, but don't feel obliged to save this tangy punch just for then. A sunny day and a few friends is all the excuse you need. This jug-sized drink is made with hibiscus tea sharpened with balsamic vinegar and a hit of fiery fizz from ginger beer. Hibiscus tea has a vibrant red colour and a tart flavour that's similar to cranberries. It's made from the petals of a hibiscus plant that's native to the Caribbean. Teaming it with vinegar and ginger creates a fizzy sweet treat of a drink that's very soothing on hot days. When you're making this summer punch use a good-quality balsamic vinegar – the syrupy kind that's as good poured over vanilla ice cream as it is drizzled on salad.

Pop the hibiscus flowers in a heatproof jug and cover with the boiling water. Set aside to steep for 10–15 minutes, then strain the tea and leave to cool. Discard the flowers. When you're ready to make the Midsummer Punch, pour the cooled hibiscus tea into a jug. Add the balsamic vinegar and the orange flower water, then drop in a couple of handfuls of sliced fruit and cucumber with a handful of fresh mint sprigs. Set aside for 15–30 minutes to infuse.

To serve, add a handful of ice and top up with chilled ginger beer. Stir a few times to mix. Serve in Collins glasses with extra ice.

# Midwinter Sparkler

**SERVES 6–8**

25g (1oz) dried hibiscus flowers
1 litre (1.7 pints) boiling water
300ml (10fl oz) Ginger Switchel (see page 21)
60ml (2fl oz) fresh lime juice
100ml (3½fl oz) Sugar-free Syrup (see page 15)
Chilled sparkling water, to top up
Lime wedges, to garnish

**If you're throwing a festive party and fancy a change from the usual mulled drinks and eggnogs served at holiday get-togethers, try this lightly sparkling punch instead. It's made with hibiscus tea, a tisane made with dried flowers that has a sweet-and-sharp berry-ish flavour. Stirred over ice with fresh lime juice and fiery Ginger Switchel, it makes an intensely plummy punch. I've used a homemade Sugar-free Syrup to add sweetness. (It's made with Xylitol and the recipe is on page 15.) If you prefer, you can swap in regular Simple Syrup (see page 15), or try a syrup flavoured with lemon or orange zest to add an extra layer of citrus brightness. This recipe is easily doubled or tripled if you want to make it for a crowd. You can mix together the hibiscus tea, lime juice, switchel, and syrup the day before and keep the mix chilled in the fridge. When your guests arrive, pour the mix into jugs, add ice and sparkling water, then get ready for the compliments. Everyone will love this chic winter sparkler..**

Pop the hibiscus flowers in a heatproof jug and cover with the boiling water. Set aside to steep for 10–15 minutes, then strain it and set aside the tea to cool. Discard the flowers. When you're ready to make the Midwinter Sparkler, add a few handfuls of ice to a jug or punch bowl. Pour in the hibiscus tea. Add the Ginger Switchel, lime juice and the Sugar-free Syrup. Stir well to mix, then top up with sparkling water. Serve in tumblers or punch cups with extra ice, garnished with lime wedges.

**Note:** If you are planning to make several batches of a drink for a party using this Sugar-free Syrup, it might be best to use Simple Syrup (see page 15) in a 1:1 swap.

# I Am The Eggnog

**SERVES 4**

4 medium eggs
115g (3¾oz) caster sugar
½ vanilla pod
250ml (8½fl oz) full-cream milk
250ml (8½fl oz) double cream
Grated nutmeg, to garnish

**Combining the vanilla richness of custard with the marshmallow fluff of meringue, these zero-proof eggnogs will be a hit with Christmas party guests who want to indulge in a festive tipple but without the fuzzy effect of all that booze. Eggnogs have been cheering up winter since the thirteenth century, although they've been through a few evolutions since the medieval mix of hot ale curdled with milk and spices kept travellers warm at coaching inns around England. These days we prefer our eggnogs to be extravagantly creamy, delicately spiced with nutmeg and definitely not curdled in any way. This version is light and airy, thanks to the egg whites that are whisked until thick then folded through a sweetened mix of cream, milk and egg yolks. It's smooth and luxurious at first sip, although the eggnog will slowly separate into a downy layer of egg white floating on a silky pool of spiced cream. You can stir them back together, or just drink the richer layer through the fluff and maybe get yourself an eggnog moustache while you're at it.**

Separate the eggs, popping the yolks into a mixing bowl and keeping the egg whites in a tub for later. Add 75g (2½oz) of the sugar to the egg yolks. Scrape the seeds from the half vanilla pod into the bowl. Use electric beaters to beat the egg yolks, vanilla and sugar together until they're thick and pale, and the beaters leave trails in the mix. Stir in the milk and cream. Pour into a sterilized bottle or jar, seal and store in the fridge until you're ready to serve – the eggnog mix will keep overnight if you want to make it ahead.

When you're ready to assemble the eggnogs, pour the reserved egg whites into a large, clean, non-plastic bowl and add the remaining 40g (1¼oz) of the sugar.

Use electric beaters to whisk them together until the egg whites are thick, opaque and form stiff peaks.

Pour the eggnog mixture into the egg whites and use a spatula to fold together until combined. Ladle the eggnog into tumblers or punch cups and grate over a little nutmeg to serve.

# Winter Cup

**SERVES 4–6**

2 English breakfast tea bags or 3 tbsp tea leaves
250ml (8½fl oz) boiling water
750ml (1.3 pints) pomegranate juice
1 orange
1 lemon
1 lime
6 whole cloves
2 cinnamon sticks
2 star anise
75ml (2½fl oz) Simple Syrup (see page 15)

**Pomegranate juice is good for you because...**

...it may help lower your blood pressure. A 2013 study found that participants who drank 150ml (5¼fl oz) pomegranate juice every day for two weeks showed a significant drop in blood pressure (in the short-term at least – the science jury is still out on the long-term effects). Study participants also reported feeling more enthusiastic and less distressed after drinking the juice, which may be another reason to crack open a pomegranate and start juicing.

**A fruity mulled punch, brimming with citrus and spice, is a festive party must-have. The scent of cinnamon and cloves is as good as a Christmas tree and fairy lights for creating a holiday atmosphere, and if it's cold outside guests are always glad to wrap their hands around a warm mug of something mulled. Even if it's not chilly, a mulled punch is still a crowd pleaser. I've used a mix of English breakfast tea and pomegranate juice in this alcohol-free version. The tea is steeped for 20 minutes to make sure it's strongly brewed, which gives it a robust tannic flavour. Combined with tart pomegranate juice, it makes a rich, gutsy stand-in for red wine. This recipe serves four to six people, but it's easily doubled, tripled or even quadrupled if you have a pan – and party – big enough.**

Make the tea by putting the tea bags or tea leaves in a heatproof jug, pour over the boiling water and leave to steep for 15 minutes to make a really strong brew.

Strain the tea and discard the tea bags or leaves. Pour the tea and the pomegranate juice into a pan. Slice the orange, lemon and lime. Stud a couple of the fruit slices with the cloves, then add them all to the pan. Drop in the cinnamon sticks and star anise. Set the pan over a medium heat, pop on a lid and bring to the boil, then turn the heat down and simmer for 10 minutes to infuse the flavours. Pour in the Simple Syrup, stir and taste. Add a little more syrup if you think it needs it. Ladle the warm Winter Cup into heatproof glasses or mugs and serve.

# Peach & Basil Smash

**SERVES 4**

For the peach and basil purée:
**200g (7oz) ripe peaches**
**Boiling water, to cover**
**15g (½oz) basil sprigs**
**2 tbsp caster sugar**
**100ml (3½fl oz) water**

To make the drinks:
**2 tsp Lapsang Souchong tea leaves**
**200ml (7fl oz) boiling water**
**60ml (2fl oz) fresh lemon juice**
**4 tsp Honey Syrup (see page 17)**
**Basil sprigs, to garnish**

**Like a midsummer bonfire on a fine June evening, this cooling zero-proof cocktail is full of smoke and sunshine. The smoke comes from the Lapsang Souchong tea. After picking, the black tea leaves are dried over pinewood fires, giving them a pungent fireside-and-cigars flavour. Shaking Lapsang Souchong with a delicate peach and basil purée rounds out the flavours, bringing out some of the tea's creamier notes, and adding a fragrant fruity smoothness. This isn't too sweet, in spite of the peach purée; the tannins in the tea take care of that. But it is a very refreshing drink. I think of it as an update on the sweet iced teas that are served in Virginia on humid summer days.**

Pop the peaches in a heatproof bowl and pour over enough boiling water to cover them. Set aside for 5 minutes, then drain the peaches and pull off the skins – the hot water should have loosened them so they just slip off. Roughly chop the peaches, discarding the stones. Pop the peaches in a small pan with the basil, sugar and water. Cover the pan with a lid, set over a medium heat and bring to a gentle boil. Turn the heat down and simmer for 3–5 minutes until the peaches are soft and collapsing. Let the peaches cool for a few minutes, then blitz the peaches, basil and their syrup in a blender or use a stick blender to blitz them in the pan. You should get a pourable peach and basil purée. If it's too thick, add a splash more water to thin it out. If you want to keep the peach purée overnight, stir in a dash of lemon juice, transfer to a tub and seal.

Tip the Lapsang Souchong tea leaves into a heatproof jug, pour over the boiling water and steep for 5 minutes. Strain the tea and discard the leaves.

If you have a large cocktail shaker, you can make two Smashes at the same time. Otherwise, shake each cocktail separately. For each Peach & Basil Smash, measure 50ml (1¾fl oz) peach and basil purée into a cocktail shaker and add 50ml (1¾fl oz) of the cooled brewed tea, 15ml (½fl oz) of the lemon juice and 1 teaspoon of the Honey Syrup. Add a handful of ice, seal the shaker and shake well for 30 seconds or so to chill. Fill an Old Fashioned glass with ice cubes and strain in the Peach & Basil Smash. Tuck in a small basil sprig to garnish. Repeat to make three more Smashes and serve.

# Blackberry Royale

**SERVES 20**

1 barley tea bag
1 litre (1.7 pints) cold water
600ml (20fl oz) Blackberry & Bay Cordial (see page 20)
1.6 litres (3½ pints) sparkling water, chilled
Blackberries, to garnish

**A celebratory drink that's perfect for toasting those extra special moments in life, this gently sparkling drink is a happy marriage of Japanese barley tea with a luscious Blackberry & Bay Cordial (you'll find the recipe on page 20). For this alcohol-free cocktail I've suggested cold brewing the barley tea for around 2 hours. This gives the tea a nice, rounded flavour, and it's ready to turn into a Blackberry Royale straight away – no need to wait for it to cool. If you want to make this cocktail for a crowd, measure out the tea and blackberry cordial into the glasses, stir together and set aside, ready to top up with chilled sparkling water just before serving.**

Pop the tea bag in a jug and top up with the cold water. Set aside for 2 hours to infuse, then discard the tea bag and pop the barley tea in the fridge to chill.

When you're ready to make the Blackberry Royale, you can either make it in a punch bowl by pouring in the cordial and tea, then topping up with sparkling water, or pour 30ml (1fl oz) Blackberry & Bay Cordial and 50ml (1¾fl oz) barley tea into each flute glass, then top up with chilled sparkling water. Gently stir to mix, drop a blackberry or two into each glass and serve.

# Index